99-1666 $24.00

I0812248

Let the People Sing!

A Keyboardist's Creative and Practical Guide to Engaging God's People in Meaningful Song

David M. Cherwien

CONCORDIA PUBLISHING HOUSE • SAINT LOUIS

3558 S. Jefferson Ave., St. Louis, MO 63118-3968
1-800-325-3040 • www.cph.org

Manufactured in the United States of America

8 9 10 11 12 13 14 15 16 24 23 22 21 20 19

Table of Contents

Part I: BASICALLY SPEAKING
Getting beyond a yawn

Part II: SERIOUSLY IMPROVISING

Getting beyond the notes on the page

Part I

BASICALLY SPEAKING...

Getting beyond a yawn

INTRODUCTION

Some of us are old enough to remember with amazement the first time we saw color television after years of seeing only black and white. The picture was the same, but with more life; more detail than we had seen before. Surroundings came alive in color, as did a new sense of focus.

In the church there are many ways that those who help the congregation sing (most often the organist) can greatly enhance the expression of the people in song. There are the basic ways: unifying the tempo, rhythm and key; assisting with the melody; bringing out the nature of the melody; and, helping the people breathe. When these aren't right, we hinder rather than help.

It is the role of "turning on the color," however, that I find increasingly important and shockingly neglected. The musician's treatment of ***text and melody*** through the introduction, the harmonic and rhythmic accompaniment, and through instrumentation and registration of the organ, has a large effect on how the congregation is encouraged to sing. Musicians have the opportunity, now more than ever, to provide a variety that continually strives for meaning, for freshness, for deeper insights.

Ours is an age of global and stylistic broadening. It is not the first such era, and likely not the last. We are stretching as a church (as we should), and are not yet quite sure how to react. No longer does all church music come from northern Europe, the primary source of professional music training. And since many traditional aspects of church music—namely, freedom, creativity and improvisation—have been forgotten or ignored in North America, musicians find themselves ill-prepared to deal with the improvisatory nature of much non-Western music. Both Northern European and non-western music have places in the music of the Church, and musicians can learn valuable lessons from both traditions. Drums of Africa can teach us about improvisation. (Conversely, the drums of Africa can also teach us about the need for counterpoint!) Perhaps the first psalmists could have taught us about freedom, since the melodies to these songs originally may have been improvised. Most classically trained musicians in North America do not practice its use. Hymns and songs from other places and times often cry out for something other than a four-part setting or for instrumentation other than organ.[1] Four-part settings are indeed important. It is important that hymnals provide them, and it is important that accompanists know how to provide them, and it is important for musicians to study them, for through them come a foundational understanding of harmony and voice-leading. There is no law, however, that says that accompanists must use them with all songs (unless the people are singing in four parts). In fact, there certainly is no law that says all congregational song has to be accompanied as Alice Parker proves every time she leads a hymn festival. She uses three things: a music stand, a hymnal, and a congregation's voice. No instruments. As accompanists we haven't learned yet how to do something other than "play" the printed four parts yet, nor what other options might be if not provided in accompaniment editions! We must learn to look beyond the page. Options need to be considered that are not typically provided in accompaniment editions.

---

[1]Having said that, I also want to be sure to say that I still believe that the organ is one of the best instruments for helping larger gatherings in song (large being more than 10.) It produces tone in the same way as the human voice—air vibrating through a tube. It can evoke the fullest praise and the quietest prayer, without the need for amplification. It also provides for the largest variety of instrumentation within one instrument! However, the use of organ for all music does not make sense. For Hispanic or Caribbean music, to use two examples, percussion-based instruments are far more helpful. However, if we don't learn to be more interesting with the organ, it may go the way of the typewriter.

In the North American context, classical musicians are often in bondage to the ink on the page. Their training looks primarily to recreating or imitating that which previously has been done. There is such a dependency on published notes that, to many musicians, the thought of changing even one note is terribly frightening and considered impossible.

On the other hand, jazz, rock, and pop musicians often don't know as much about construction, form, or the gravitational pulls of musical nature and theory—the knowledge of which could open up tremendous freedoms! What they do develop is a repertoire of "licks," rhythmic and harmonic nuances that they may have heard or discovered along the way, and they know how to plug them into an accompaniment appropriately. They are freer to interact spontaneously with the others with whom they are making music—constantly giving and receiving ideas from each other as they make the music. It is unique to that moment, and rarely exactly the same the next time.

We must learn this freedom in all church music—we need to loosen up. I carry with me a philosophy from my rock-band days: the tune and its lyrics were the given. What we did under and around them was always up for grabs. We were always in search of a more interesting chord or rhythmic motive. It was rarely the same twice, yet very recognizable to the listener. In following this principle in worship, the congregation's song is able to be unique to this time, this context, custom fit to these people on this day. No publisher or composer can know our congregation, its hymn repertoire, the worship space and its acoustics, the instruments and instrumentalists, choirs and pastors, better than we its musicians.[2] When modern church musicians can learn how to look beyond turning every congregational song into a four-part German chorale regardless of its origins, (as Alice Parker teaches,) we can learn more about how the growing diversity of the hymns and songs of God's people in worship can blossom more fully in their natural way.

Simultaneously, as the church's musical "prophets in their midst," if we espouse freedom, it should not be "willy-nilly," or merely what "feels right." Musicians must know the construction of their craft and control it. It's nice to be able to see what the fingers provide by chance and intuition, but leave it at that and we limit the potential or wind up with chaos. Following the rock band days I studied liturgical improvisation in Berlin, Germany. It was not acceptable to merely let my fingers go where they wanted in hopes of a good sound. I had to include my brain! I had to learn to see ahead and *tell* my fingers where to go, to weed out redundancies and weaknesses by learning to see them coming, and by analytically hearing them. It's hard to see the flowers when the garden is full of weeds. Understanding harmony and voice-leading provided more freedom with much more clarity and control.

Musicians need to bridge the intuitive and the sensate, striving for a balance between the two. We are free to help a text grow through its music beyond what is printed with it on the page, yet fully aware of the structure. In balancing improvisational freedom with structural discipline we enable and nourish congregational song.

But how? Where? Where to start? When to draw the line? How do we decide in what manner to treat a given song?

---

[2]Bach operated this way as a part of the routine. Most likely when he had a good soprano and trumpet player, he'd compose something like Cantata 51, "Jauchzet Gott in allen Landen" for soprano and trumpet!

This book seeks to deal with these questions. It begins with that which anyone can do right away directly from this book to the keyboard, and it also includes that which involves time and practice.

All that falls between the covers however, seeks this:

> To give the people permission to sing out, and to give them permission to sing with deeper meaning.

This is not a superimposed meaning by the musicians, but a meaning that we can allow the congregation to cut loose with on their own. Musicians show the people the button for the color; the people get to turn it on.

I have chosen to write the book in a casual conversational style—as if leading a workshop. My hope is that you, like I, continue to enjoy the humor of life as we together shrug our shoulders and try something new. In other words, we seek to carry out the very serious responsibility with a sense of humor.

Chapter I

BE CLEAR!

...catch my vibes?

THE NATURE OF SINGING

This book is for those who help congregations sing, in most situations, a keyboard accompanist, usually an organist. But before I begin with the "how-to" stylebook for keyboard accompanists, a discussion about the nature of singing is in order. To be the most effective instigators of congregational song, we must be truly sympathetic to the singers in the pews—to put ourselves in their pews, so to speak.

It is an astounding thing that people sing in church. We are given only one voice in life and it is a deep part of us that we can't exchange for another. We certainly can learn how to use it better, but nevertheless it is the same voice we were born with. To use it in public song is to expose a part of us that we don't expose willy-nilly to anyone. I'm sure some folks would rather run in public stark naked than sing in public.

It makes sense to sing, as it is a natural and healing act, and is quite the release. Babies first sing at birth...(talk about release!). As Paul Westermeyer says:

> The human race is driven to sing. As Joseph Gelineau points out: Babies cry. We need help, so we shout. A friend dies, and we weep. We writhe in pain and groan. Or, the baby prattles. The lover whistles. We are happy, and we hum. We hear a joke, and we laugh. Those are all incipiently musical activities.
>
> In groups we are driven to sing. We sing at someone's birthday. When a war ends, people shout out their national anthem.[1]

And it makes sense to sing in church. We let go and share a deep part of ourselves with God and each other, and we accept the gifts of the voices around us joined to ours. We join with each other in a very real way, as all music is vibration. When we sing, we literally vibrate together—either in unison or in harmony. Even the harmonies most often sung are a furthering of unison, as most of these consonant intervals are a natural part of the harmonic series. Rhythmic unity carries this farther—we sing in the same pulse (even if in syncopation). We are scientifically "catching each other's vibes," becoming one voice.

Other than in church, there are very few places in people's lives where they sing. At ball games a group or soloist is hired to sing the national anthem into the sound system, and the crowd stands hands on hearts and silently listens, or at best sort of mumbles the words as they are sung by the professionals. The most often cited location for singing is in the shower. (No surprise; there's rarely carpeting in there to soak up the sound.) It doesn't get any more intimate than in the shower!

Yet in worship, we sing. Astounding!

---

[1]Westermeyer, Paul, "To Be Human Is to Sing," *The Luther Northwestern Story,* (Winter 1990). Used by permission.

Add to all this that ours is not an age of participatory music-making, and it is an age of musical perfection. People's contact with music is most often prerecorded playback with perfect studio-adjusted balance, musical perfection without knowing how many "takes" it took for that difficult section. The next most frequent contact with music is in the concert hall—well-rehearsed professional performances, jazz, rock or classical. Rarely does anyone gather for informal music-making, as was often the case in history. The electronic age has changed all that.

The church's song is much different from these examples. It is an entirely different beast, and we shouldn't try to imitate the music people come into contact with outside the church when facilitating music for use in worship. Music in the church, especially that which the congregation sings, has its own unique character. Music of the church is mostly corporate song, as opposed to entertainment-based music, which makes up the majority of the music in our modern secular culture. Awareness of the differences between secular music and music of the church, however, does inform us for our task of encouraging the people to sing.

My favorite example of group singing is the ritual song "Happy Birthday." People don't go in search of a soloist, choir director, or accompanist in order to sing it. People don't even seem to worry about being on pitch or about what key in which to sing it. It is merely a heartfelt wish for happiness sung to friends and family on the anniversary of their birth.

This is the climate I strive for in the congregation—true hospitality in which there is absence of fear of judgment; true, simple and natural communal expression in song.

We song leaders, accompanists, organists can help create this atmosphere. And we can do the reverse—we can damage or even destroy it.

THE DFA SYNDROME

Doubt to Fear to Abstinence

The number one congregational song inhibitor is **DOUBT**, ("Are we supposed to sing now?") , which leads to **FEAR**, ("Am I going to get caught singing a solo?"), which leads to **ABSTINENCE**, (I'd rather run in public naked!). If the space between phrases is unclear, and Joe the brickmaker comes in early, he'll never sing again. If people are not sure when the next stanza begins, they will wait for someone else to start first, which gradually decreases the tempo of the song. If the organist plays too quietly people will assume that there is a soloist who will pop out of the closet to sing that stanza, and they will remain silent. If the harmony put under the melody is so strange that the next notes of the melody are hard to find, people will not sing. If there is no time to breathe, they won't sing the first couple of notes. If the tempo varies, people will get quieter in hopes that someone else will find the tempo first.

There are many ways in which doubt can be created. Actually, all that follows in this entire book should beg this question: "Could what I'm doing as accompanist be raising doubt?" If so, it should not be done. I would like to start with some basic doubt-bashers. Remember that people don't sing just anywhere and would rather be found dead than sing a solo in public. If you raise doubt, forcing people to risk *the solo,* they are not going to sing.

It is vital that the downbeat always be reliable, predictable and consistent. People know they can breathe and sing out on the downbeat without wondering if they are going to be alone. There are a number of things which can put the downbeat at risk.

TACTUS

Is it clear and consistent? *Tactus* sounds like a high-brow word. It means "pulse." It could also be thought of as the bottom number of the time signature. 4/4 means four beats per measure—the quarter note getting the beat. But one could also think 2/2, or 1/1. Is your pulse clear? Does it remain consistent? There is no one correct pulse for most hymns. Your space, your people, your instrument, and even the context in which the hymn is placed can render a different understanding of pulse. Take for example, "Holy, Holy, Holy." Set a metronome to ♩ = 88 and sing, clapping at the X.

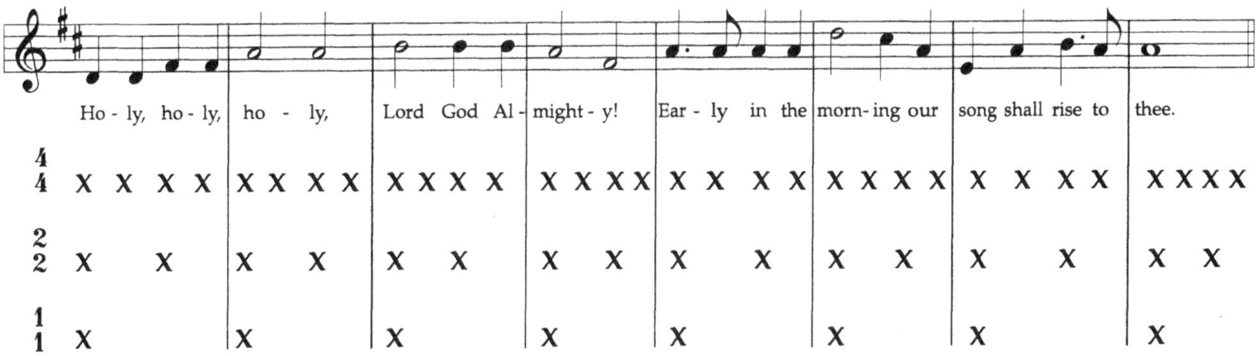

Example 1.1. "Holy, Holy, Holy," Text: Reginald Heber, 1783–1826, alt. Tune: NICAEA, John B. Dykes, 1823–76.

Notice how 1/1 "feels" slower, even though it is in reality the same "speed."

Which is correct? That is your job to decide! If it is a majestic processional hymn (as its Anglican origin might suggest), 4/4 makes more sense with its broad march feel. But if it is the closing hymn of an hour-and-a-half service (which started at 11:00 a.m.), and you choose 4/4, people will think about lunch rather than singing of the majesty of God.

Decide on the hymn's tactus for that day and time of day, point in the service, acoustics, number of people, etc., and stick to it. Do not experiment by playing it at the keyboard; do it by singing away from the keyboard. Which tactus provides a natural flow, allowing you to sing the words unrushed and naturally but in a way that you are able to sing an entire phrase without an injection of oxygen? Which tactus highlights the natural rhythm of an entire phrase? Prepare this in advance, not during the service.

Some types of hymns are non-metric, and do not have a regular tactus, such as Gregorian chant tunes. I believe a pulse still exists; it just isn't regular. It occurs on a "downbeat" of each phrase, letting the remainder of the phrase float like a feather in the air. The "downbeat" is the puff of air that sends it back up. The breath is the cue for all to sing together with these hymns. More about breath shortly.

During the service, be consistently clear about where the downbeats and/or tactus lie. Monitor how the people are doing with them. If in the course of the song the tactus comes into question, for example, if the congregation and choir get off, it is your job to bring them back together. Detach from chord to chord until it is reunified. Conduct the choir to match the congregation. Play louder until reunited. Whatever it takes, bring it back in sync.

Ritardandi and rubati also need to be avoided, as they throw off the tactus and put the downbeat in question. Ritards perhaps can come in only at the very end of the last stanza, yet in ways that are natural, gradual, and vocal. When done, ritards should be clear, and not too sudden. In the case of ritards, think of the congregational song as a long and heavy train. Sudden starts and stops are not possible. They cause train wrecks.

BREATH. Allow for it, but not in ways that interrupt the tactus. Breath always must come from the previous beat, so that the down beat remains on time. (Remember, if the downbeat is not consistently on time, it raises the DFA syndrome.) But for heaven's sake, allow for breath!

WARNING! Insufficient or inconsistent breath allowance may be injurious to the health of congregational song, and may even lead to death thereof.

There are two different types of breathing points to consider: leading into stanzas and between phrases within stanzas. In either case, the overarching question is the same: "Where is the downbeat?" When the breath leading to the downbeat is clear, singing happens without fear.

THE ALL-IMPORTANT BREATH LEADING INTO STANZAS

This is an important breath, as it communicates the start of the tactus, which informs people where the downbeat is.

Organists as a rule do not breathe enough at this point, and I mean physically take in air themselves! To truly understand how much space is needed, you must actually take in air. Watch conductors some time. When THEY give the upbeat, they always breathe. If they don't, the choir or orchestra does not believe the downbeat.

The breath before the first stanza is of great importance. It signals the end of the introduction and gives the upbeat for the congregation to breathe before singing the first note. The *breath* here does more to signal the end of the introduction than a fermata, ritard or any other musical signal used at the end of the keyboard introduction. If the breath is unclear, the start will also be unclear. This, I believe, is most often the cause of congregations' objections to free introductions—the keyboardist is unclear about when the introduction is done, and therefore unclear about *when people are to breathe.* People fear the solo and blame the free-introduction rather than the unclear breath. More about that in a later chapter.

There are many theories about this breath. Some have taught systems like adding so many beats, measures, etc., most of which strive to maintain the tactus. While that may indeed work, the believable upbeat is the most important factor. The clearest breath signal is the all-limbs-off-the-keyboard-silence.

Whether we stay metrical or not, I believe it takes **two moments** to signal a breath. A "moment" I consider to be one beat within the "tactus." The first one is for people to notice the silence (reactionary moment), the second is the breath itself. Most often the second of the two is eliminated. People tend to have to breathe on the downbeat when they are supposed to be singing, or take a stab breath, breathing out of tactus. Often I hear a very long fermata to signal the end of the introduction, but only one moment for the breath. One moment feels fine to the keyboard player, but is not enough for the singers in the pews unless they are mind readers. Use the all-limbs-off-the-keyboard-silence. It works!

With "one" moment:

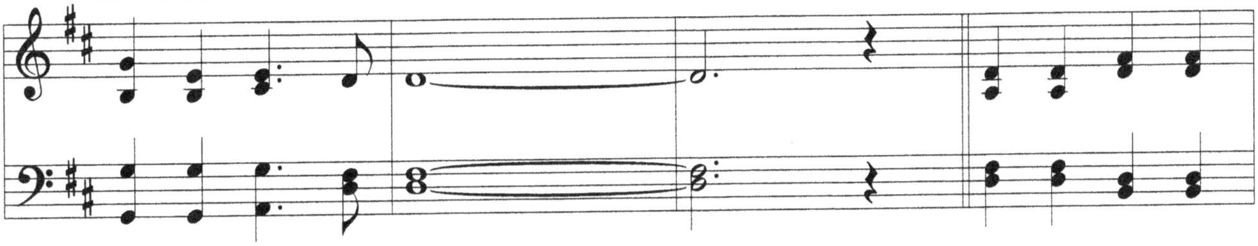

Example 1.2. "Holy, Holy, Holy," Tune: NICAEA, John B. Dykes, 1823–76.

With "two" moments:

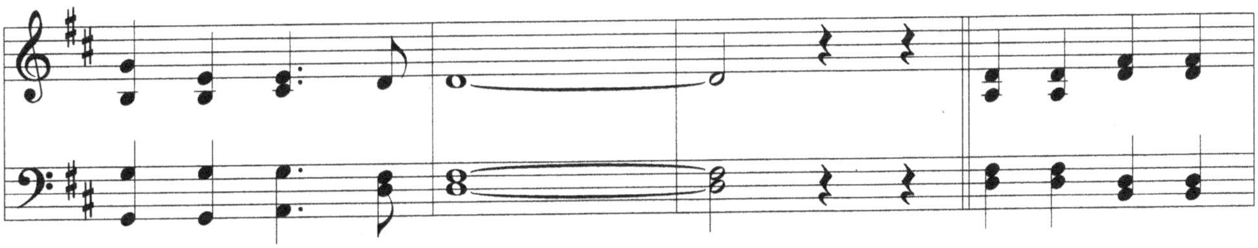

Example 1.3. "Holy, Holy, Holy," Tune: NICAEA, John B. Dykes, 1823–76.

BREATH BETWEEN PHRASES

Here things are more simple. Steal the breath from the previous beat without interrupting the tactus so that the downbeat after the breath is right on time. How much space to steal for a breath? Try *singing* it yourself to answer that question. Try singing it with a metronome to duplicate the bulldozer effect of congregational song, and to be sure the tactus is not interrupted. Do, however, get used to the "all-limbs-off-the-keyboard-silence." It is the clearest breath signal, but the most awkward when we are practicing, as that silence is quite uncomfortable. Remember that the most important piece of the puzzle is missing in the practicing context—the congregation.

Sometimes there are not-so-clear breath spots for us to deal with. In the metrical version of "Now Thank We All Our God," there is only a quarter-note at the end of the first full phrase.

Example 1.4. "Now Thank We All Our God," Text: Martin Rinkhart, tr. Catherine Winkworth, 1829–78.
Tune: NUN DANKET ALLE GOTT, Johann Crüger, 1598–1662.

Resist the fermata! That stops the tactus and makes the continuance uncertain for the people without a visual conductor. The last quarter-note has to become quite short for the organist, in order to continue reliably. It may be possible to stretch the breath ever so slightly to make room for a good breath, but not so much as to throw the tactus into question. Practice this with your voice, not with your limbs on a keyboard. Some hymnals deal with these spots by simply printing a longer note-value and changing the time signature for that measure. I find this awkward, because the downbeat on paper becomes counter to nature.

As a side note, consider with this particular example how changing the original version can create problems. This hymn in its original form is non-metrical and dance-like in its rhythm. Squaring it off into 4/4 creates this breathing problem. More about that later....

WITH ONE VOICE

One Unifier, please.

Picture this: A hymn is under way, yet there seem to be several leaders: the organist who is playing; the choir director who is trying to slow down the tempo; a pastor who is trying to pep it up through loud singing; a loud singing congregational member who loves hymns the way they sang them as a child—fermatas, rubato and all; and a section of the choir two beats ahead of everyone else totally unaware.

Been there? Done that?

Who are the people supposed to follow? If this is in question, the DFA syndrome arises. And, if the congregation is to be "one voice" in song, there can only be one unifier. One tactus needs to prevail to keep the breathing and downbeat reliable; one key needs to prevail for obvious reasons. There may be as many different opinions about such matters as there are worshipers, but I feel this responsibility needs to be designated to one source for the sake of the congregational song, and not by reason of power issues. The cantor—the leader of the people's song—has this office. And the cantor among us most often is the organist. In some situations someone else may lead, such as a cantor in many Roman Catholic parishes—a visible singer in the front, a conductor for the congregation. In some settings it may indeed be the best stewardship of the congregation's song for that leader to be the pastor. Only one tactus needs to prevail, for clarity and for unity's sake.

Onward Christian singers! The basics have been covered. The vegetables and healthy foods have been considered. If these things are unclear to you, do not proceed.

Now, on to the "color."

Chapter 2

GREETINGS!

...the hymn introduction

When you see someone you know while out for a walk, how do you greet that person? If you say in a sullen, lethargic tone and a serious face, "Hi," the response will most likely be in similar fashion: "Hi; what's wrong?" If you say an enthusiastic "Hello!" with a smile, the response will duplicate the enthusiasm. When the accompanist introduces a hymn in a lethargic fashion, you can guess what the people will do. If the accompanist always introduces every hymn the same way, you can guess what the people will do. Yet, the texts that we sing are tremendously varied! Consider these two texts, which in one hymnal use the same tune:

Hallelujah! Jesus lives!
He is now the Living One;
From the gloomy halls of death
Christ, the conqueror, has gone,
Bright forerunner to the skies
Of his people, yet to rise.

Carl B. Garve, 1763–1841, tr. Jane Borthwick, 1813–97.

Peace to soothe our bitter woes
God in Christ on us bestows;
Jesus bought our peace with God
With his holy, precious blood;
Peace in him for sinners found
Is the Gospel's joyful sound

Nikolai F. S. Grundtvig, 1783–1872, tr. George T. Rygh, 1860–1943.

Imagine if we introduced these two texts in the exact same way. It would not encourage the meaning of these very different texts. The first should call for full orchestra, but in the second, the word "peace" wants to jump off the page—but not with trumpets.

If we are to allow the meaning of a hymn to be fully expressed, we need to give the congregation permission to express it. If it is full praise, the introduction should announce that. If it is quiet prayer, the introduction should announce that. If we are afraid to use the full organ, even though the text says "PRAISE God **ALL** creatures here below...," the people will in like fashion be afraid to use their full voices. And, if we do not use quiet sounds, we say to them it is not acceptable to sing quietly, even though the text says "O little town of Bethlehem, how **STILL** we see thee lie!..." (I have found over the years that singing quietly is often more difficult to encourage than singing loudly.) The introductions must give permission for the hymn to be sung with meaning.

WARNING! Blah introductions beget blah singing, and the use thereof may increase the blah factor of the congregation!

PREPARING THE INTRODUCTION

There are many things a hymn accompanist must consider when preparing each hymn for worship. Alice Parker keeps reminding us to "read the small print" about the music of the hymn. Where does the tune come from? How might it have sounded there and then? What are the rhythms; what is the melody; what is the tactus? Certainly the introduction needs to bring these out. Alice Parker does this verbally and by vocal example; accompanists do it through the music of the introduction.

A thorough reading and studying of the text—**all of the stanzas**—is also of great importance. What does the poetry of the text mean? How does it fit into the context of the service in which the hymn is placed? These findings are extremely important and can especially be brought out in the introduction.

The preparation process should begin away from the keyboard.

While studying with Paul Manz, I was introduced to a process that I have cherished and used since. Permit me to share it with you.

To decide how I am going to introduce a hymn, I must first understand how I might suggest to the congregation to sing it—and what may be brought out in the text given the context in which the hymn is placed. That may include reading the scripture lessons for that particular service, and certainly knowing what precedes and follows the hymn in the service.

From there, I then read all the stanzas of the hymn and underline a word or short phrase that captures the main point of the hymn for that service. (Here's a news flash: this often is not in the first phrase or first stanza! It amazes me how often we read the title of the hymn and base all considerations of the entire hymn text on that short phrase.) I then underline that phrase lightly in pencil and let my imagination fly: how can I paint a musical picture of that word or phrase?

For example, consider the hymn "Come, Thou Long-Expected Jesus." Imagine its context in the First Sunday in Advent, where the assigned Gospel lesson tells us, "But about that day or hour no one knows, neither the angels in heaven, nor the Son, but only the Father. Beware, keep alert; for you do not know when the time will come." (Mark 13:32-33 *NRSV*) I imagine a world that is in great need of redemption, full of our busy sins, and I underline the following phrase:

> Come, thou long-expected Jesus, Born to set thy people free;
> <u>From our fears and sins release us</u>; Let us find our rest in thee.
> Israel's strength and consolation, Hope of all the earth thou art,
> Dear desire of every nation, Joy of every longing heart.
>
> Charles Wesley, 1707–88.

And the introduction seeks to bring out that particular phrase of the text.

Example 2.1. Tune: JEFFERSON, *Southern Harmony*. Arrangement: David M. Cherwien, *Interpretations, Book IV*, © 1984. Summa Productions, Minneapolis, MN 55414-1510.

Yet the thrust of the hymn's theme that you might underline may change from use to use, or from context to context. This means that doing this process once is not permanent. One Sunday in Advent when "Come, Thou Long-Expected Jesus" immediately followed the sermon, the preacher spoke about the comfort of this promise and the joy of the "rest" on the day when Christ returns. So for that service, I underlined:

> Come, thou long-expected Jesus, Born to set thy people free;
> From our fears and sins release us; Let us find our rest in thee.
> Israel's strength and consolation, Hope of all the earth thou art,
> Dear desire of every nation, Joy of every longing heart.
>
> Charles Wesley, 1707–88.

That context told me to introduce the hymn with the following:

Example 2.2. Tune: JEFFERSON, *Southern Harmony,* Arrangement: David M. Cherwien, *Interpretations, Book VII,* © 1988. Summa Productions, Minneapolis, MN 55414-1510.

I imagine a context where I might underline "Israel's strength," where I could use reeds and a strong pulse to introduce this hymn.

There are further considerations not yet mentioned that come into play in the introduction. Is the tune known? If it is a new tune, you may need to go through the tune more than once. If it is very familiar, a few notes hinting at the tune would be sufficient. What you surround that tune with is totally up for grabs, but implied at in the textuality, and influenced by the tune's origin.

An important point, however, is that one must weigh all these things and come up with an inviting introduction that fits it all together: READ THE TEXT; think about how it might find its meaning; couple that information with the musical questions of the tune (its origin, tactus, rhythm and flow, familiarity); then let your creative juices flow freely to consider how you will introduce the hymn in a way that evokes meaningful response in the singing.

Paul Manz describes it as a circle. "I work with a text and this in turn generates for me an image, either theological or musical. I then explore that imagery in my imagination, putting musical form to it. Then when I present this at the people's song I find they are enlivened by it and this excitement returns to me through their singing and the circle is complete."[1]

The introduction is the spring board to this process.

[1]Paul Manz on his work, printed on a brochure for the Paul Manz Institute of Church Music, 1500 West Belmont Avenue, Chicago, IL. Used by permission.

ANYTHING BUT MERELY PLAYING THE FIRST AND LAST LINE!

I would venture a guess that the majority of hymn accompanists introduce the hymns by playing through them once, or by playing the first and last line. If so, one can still go through the above process and at least register the instrument accordingly. If fullness is desired, consider playing all parts on one manual with an 8′ Reed alone, or with 16′, 8′ Reeds and Mixture. If quietness is desired, consider an 8′ String and its Celeste alone, perhaps adding a 4′ Flute to them. If fullness or quietness is not the issue, at least solo out the melody with an individual stop—an 8′ or 16′ Reed, or 8′ Principal, or 4′ Flute with the accompaniment using 8′ and 4′ Flutes. In any case, you need not use the exact same sound that you will use in the accompaniment once the singing begins. Do something different!

If you are unable to do something beyond simply playing through the melody without losing the clarity of when the people are to sing, by all means continue introductions that way.

However...

I think the use of free introductions can allow so much more to happen with a hymn! The usual musical things an introduction must accomplish can still happen with free introductions: announcing the tune, tactus, and rhythm. The text and its meaning are far more effectively unleashed through free introductions. Length can be more flexible. People can be brought into the hymn more effectively by bringing out the uniqueness of every hymn sung. Since no one is singing during the introduction, why should the accompanist be bound to the notes printed in the hymnal?

Through free introductions, the organist is also able to bring out unique colors of the instrument when not playing four voices all the time. The 16′ Oboe stop all by itself, introducing the tune to "Children of the Heavenly Father," may be the only opportunity for that stop to be used and would be much more effective and interesting than playing through the tune once with the 8′ and 4′ Flutes. Since no one is singing, fewer chorus stops and more individual stops may be used. This also makes the cue to sing clearer: when the principal chorus comes on the congregation knows to sing.

There are many, many publications of organ pieces that may serve as introductions, spanning various eras of history. J. S. Bach's chorale prelude on "Liebster Jesu" in the *Orgelbüchlein* would make a beautiful introduction to the text "Dearest Jesus, we are here..." Current-day organist/composers are pumping out books of these pieces, including yours truly. Use them to introduce the hymn instead of just using such pieces for the prelude, offertory, or postlude.

17 SIMPLE SUGGESTIONS FOR FREE INTRODUCTIONS

Why not work on doing your own? After all, how can composers know your context, your people, your instrument, your preacher's emphasis? Here are some starters that you could use right off the bat, even if you have never improvised.

◆ 1. **Adding voices.** Add one voice at a time as the introduction progresses:

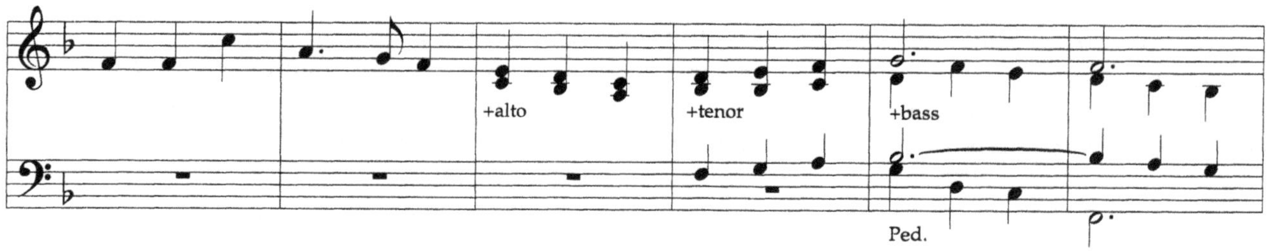

Example 2.3. "Praise to the Lord," Tune: LOBE DEN HERREN, *Ernewertes Gesangbuch*, Stralsund, 1665.

You can do this for each phrase, or spread entrances out, adding voices one phrase at a time, or vary it throughout.

◆ 2. **Alternate between unison and harmony.** Explore this process and add a coda that reiterates the opening line, adding to the suspense, and encouraging an even stronger breath just before the people finally get to sing!

Example 2.4. "Praise to the Lord," Tune: LOBE DEN HERREN.

In fact, who says that the melody always has to remain the property of the right hand? Imagine how left out the left hand and feet feel. Pass the melody around as you alternate between unison and harmony. Note in the next example that it is a good idea to "play through the rests," (between measures 5 and 6), or to shorten some cadence measures (measure 3). This serves the purpose of NOT giving the congregation the option of breathing at that moment. It's not yet time for them to sing!

Example 2.5. "A Mighty Fortress Is Our God," Tune: EIN FESTE BURG, Martin Luther, 1483–1546.

◆ 3. **Not the first phrase.** Who says the introduction has to begin with the first phrase? Especially with well-known tunes, phrases can be mixed up without throwing the congregation for a loop. This new mix may even pull them into the hymn more effectively!

Example 2.6. "Praise to the Lord," Tune: LOBE DEN HERREN.

or

Example 2.7. "Joy to the World," Tune: ANTIOCH, George F. Handel, 1685–1759.

Sometimes mixing up the phrases leads to something else:

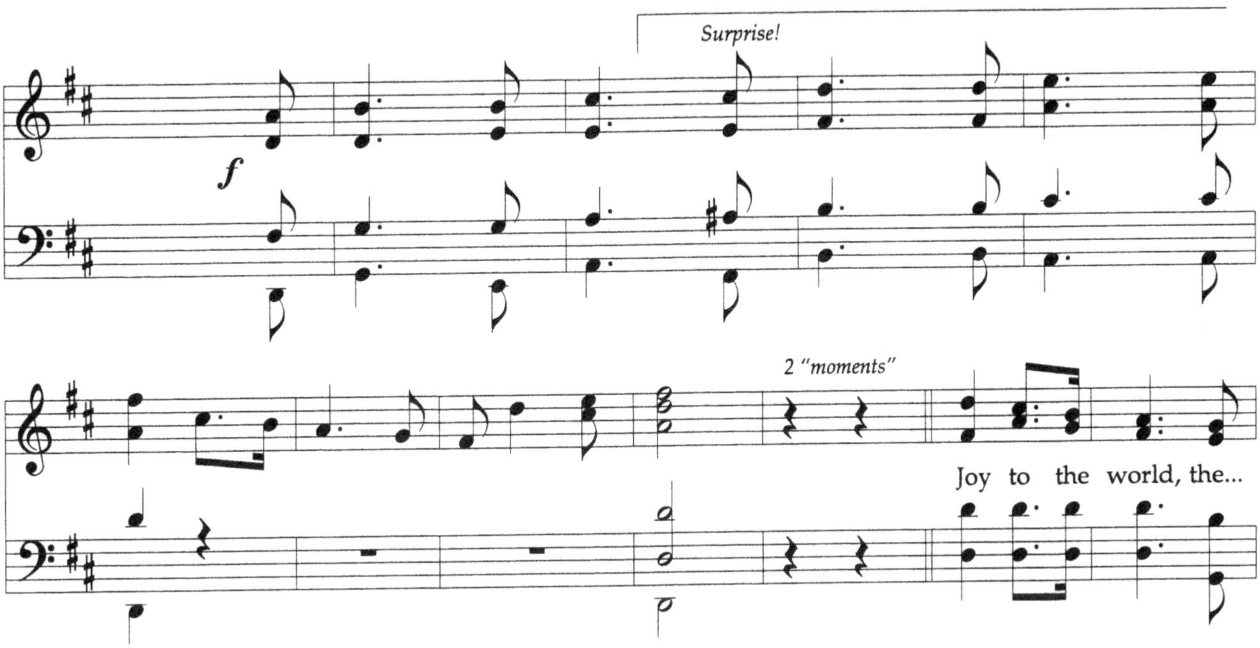

Example 2.8. "Joy to the World," Tune: ANTIOCH, George F. Handel, 1685–1759.

◆ 4. **Canon.** Start by using only two voices, one hand on one manual, the other hand on another manual with a contrasting sound. (For example, use an 8′ Reed on one manual, and 8′ and 2′ Flutes on the other.) Avoid using the same sound for both manuals, unless that is the desired effect. Note the altering of the upper voice to avoid consecutive octaves to keep the two parts distinct. Remember, no one is singing. This is OK!

Example 2.9. "Let All Mortal Flesh Keep Silence," Tune: PICARDY, French folk tune, 17th century.

Experiment with different spaces between entrances:

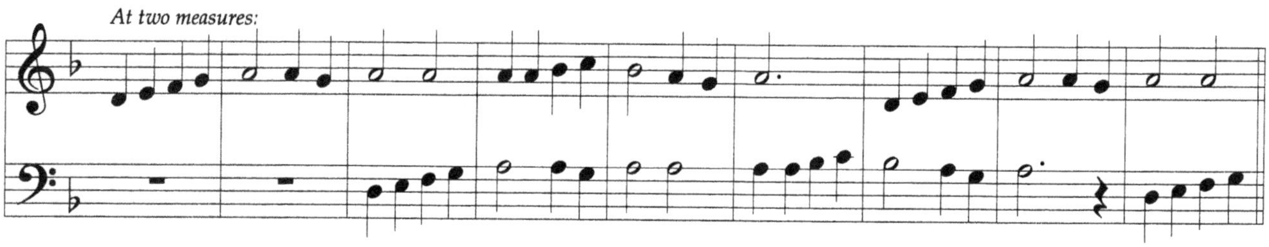

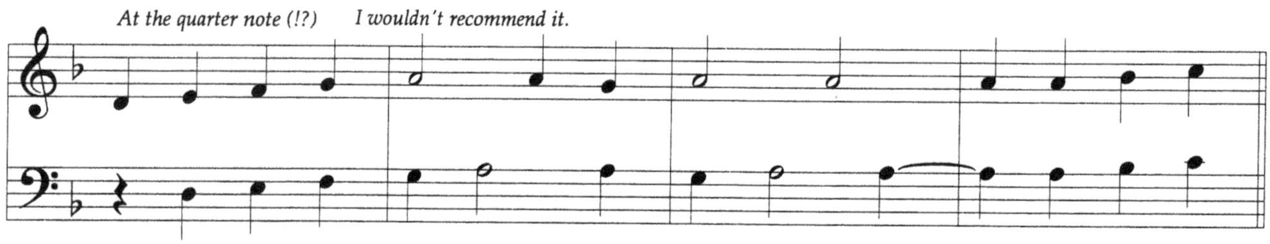

Example 2.10. "Let All Mortal Flesh Keep Silence," Tune: PICARDY, French folk tune, 17th century.

◆ 5. **Canon and harmony.** Alternate canon phrases with straight harmony out of the book:

Example 2.11. "Let All Mortal Flesh Keep Silence," Tune: PICARDY, French folk tune, 17th century.

◆ 6. **Melody as solo, without any accompanying harmony.** (Maybe even use the tremolo!) Early American tunes such as "Amazing Grace" work especially well doing this. It's the instrument's chance to let the Oboe stop be heard by itself. Perhaps you have a lovely 8′ Flute, or a 4′ Flute alone, or try the 2′ Flute played down an octave by itself. The total absence of harmony will create a wonderful suspenseful effect, relieved only when the singing begins.

◆ 7. **Pedal Point.** Plant your left foot (or a heavy book) on either the tonic or dominant and leave it there as you play through the hymn until you can't stand it any more. Then switch to the actual music for a phrase, and go back to playing a pedal point for the last phrase. Pedal points can be used to introduce loud or soft hymns! The following pedal point for the hymn "The Church's One Foundation" points out the word "foundation":

Example 2.12. "The Church's One Foundation," Tune, AURELIA, Samuel S. Wesley, 1810–76.
Text: Samuel J. Stone, 1839–1900.

Example 2.13. "O Little Town of Bethlehem," Tune: ST. LOUIS, Lewis H. Redner, 1831–1908.

◆ 8. **Ostinato pattern under the melody.**

Example 2.14. "Lord Whose Love in Humble Service," Tune: BEACH SPRING, *The Sacred Harp*, 1844, Philadelphia, PA .

Early American tunes, often pentatonic (built on steps 1,2,3,5, and 6 of the scale), work well with ostinatos built on open fifths. Perhaps an open fifth ostinato pattern can also bring out the renaissance character of a tune:

Example 2.15. "Comfort, Comfort, Now My People," Tune: FREU DICH SEHR, *Trente quatre pseaumes de David*, Geneva, 1551.

Perhaps create a longer ostinato pattern.

Example 2.16. "Prepare the Royal Highway," Tune: BEREDEN VÄG FÖR HARRAN, Swedish folk tune, 14th century. Arrangement: David M. Cherwien, *Interpretations, Book IV,* © 1984, Summa Productions, Minneapolis, MN 55414-1510.

When the pattern is tiring, simply move to a new key. I've enjoyed simply making any note of a phrase the new home key for the pattern, and simply move there without passing "go." In the case of this particular hymn introduction arrangement "Prepare the Royal Highway," I do it twice, but for the last phrase, I simply "run home" with the pattern back to G major, the home key.

Example 2.17. "Prepare the Royal Highway," Tune: BEREDEN VÄG FÖR HARRAN, Swedish folk tune, 14th century. Arrangement: David M. Cherwien, *Interpretations, Book IV,* © 1984, Summa Productions, Minneapolis, MN 55414-1510.

Ostinatos can simply be two alternating chords:

Example 2.18. "Thee We Adore, O Hidden Savior," Tune: ADORO TE DEVOTE, Mode V; *Processionale*, Paris, 1697. Arrangement: David M. Cherwien *Interpretations, Book III*, © 1983, Summa Productions, Minneapolis, MN 55414-1510.

By putting the notes of the melody in different octaves, adding passing notes, and altering the rhythm, Helmut Walcha composed a wonderful three-measure ostinato pattern which included the melody in an undercover fashion. Then he brought in the phrases of the hymn tune in unexpected places. Here's the tune:

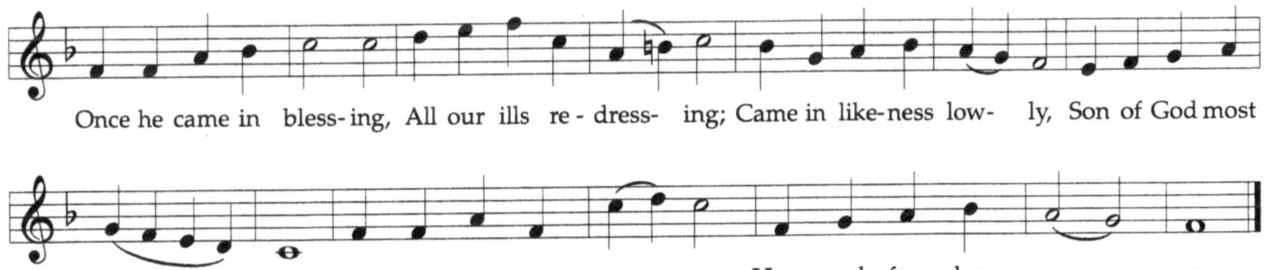

Example 2.19. "Once He Came in Blessing," Text: Johann Horn, c. 1490–1547, tr. Catherine Winkworth, 1829–78, alt. Tune: GOTTES SOHN IST KOMMEN, Bohemian Brethren, 1531. *Ein New Gesengbuchlen.*

Walcha put this tune to use in an ostinato pattern, and it became:

Example 2.20. Arrangement by Helmut Walcha, Source: H. Walcha, *Chorale Preludes, Volume II*. Edition Peters. © 1963 Henry Litolff's Verlag, C. F. Peters, Frankfurt, London, New York. Used by permission.

◆ 9. **Fanfare.** Take the notes 1 and 5 of the scale, add some dotted rhythms, and voilà! Great fanfares!

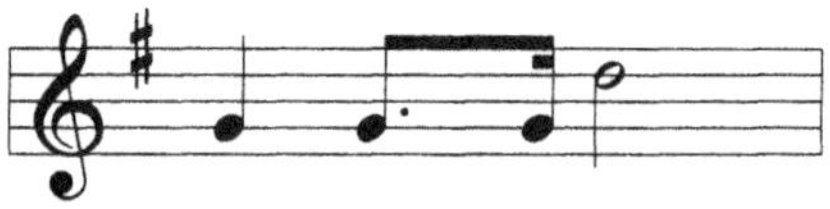

Example 2.21.

Most hymnals with the hymn "God of Our Fathers" include this "lick" right in the book. It's amazing the imagery evoked by mere triplets and a triad! Apply this to other hymns where the text may invite such a treatment. Merely insert these between phrases for an instruction:

Example 2.22. "Oh, Worship the King," Tune: HANOVER, William Croft, 1678–1727.

Add a second to the triad; alternate with a "minor dominant," and things get even more interesting:

Example 2.23. "All Hail the Power of Jesus' Name," Tune: CORONATION, Oliver Holden, 1765–1844.

◆ 10. **Use only two voices.** Dedicate one voice to the melody; allow the other voice to be totally free, striving for an occasional consonant (nice) interval such as a third, fifth, sixth, or octave/unison. As with the canon, use two contrasting sounds, the louder of the two being the melody. There are many examples of this in literature by composers such as Pachelbel, Walther, Bach, and Walcha.

Example 2.24. "Good Christian Friends, Rejoice," Tune: IN DULCI JUBILO, German carol, 14th century.

◆ 11. **Ritornello.** Imagine a simple musical thought that you play between phrases of the hymn in various keys. I invent them together with the opening phrase of the hymn by playing opposites: if the melody of the hymn goes up, the counter melody will go down; if the rhythm stands still, the counter melody will move. A detailed process for inventing these is provided in Chapter 9.

Example 2.25. "Whatever God Ordains Is Right," Tune: WAS GOTT TUT, Severus Gastorius, c. 1675.
Arrangement: David M. Cherwien, *Interpretations, Book VII,* © 1988, Summa Productions, Minneapolis, MN 55414-1510.

◆ 12. **Solo out the melody over soft stops.** Add passing tones and trills to the melody.

Example 2.26. "Ah, Holy Jesus," Tune: HERZLIEBSTER JESU, Johann Crüger, 1598–1662.

◆ 13. **Treat each phrase.** Expand on number 12, adding "introductions" to each phrase derived from the phrase itself.

Example 2.27. Tune: O WALY, WALY, English tune.

◆ 14. **Countermelody.** Expand on 13 using a "countermelody" not related to the melody itself, but derived from the text perhaps. This example, based on "Lord, Whose Love in Humble Service," uses a "humble" countermelody between phrases:

Example 2.28. "Lord, Whose Love in Humble Service," Tune: BEACH SPRING, *The Sacred Harp*, Philadelphia, PA 1884. Arrangement: David M. Cherwien, *Interpretations, Book VII*, © 1988, Summa Productions, Minneapolis, MN 55414-1510.

◆ 15. **Published Literature.** Use a published organ chorale prelude, but give the melody of the hymn to an instrumentalist in the congregation. In the previous example "Lord, Whose Love in Humble Service," give the countermelody to a flute; or give the melody itself to a flute player. (Flutes, however, often sound better on hymn melodies played up one octave. Most flute players do this instinctively. The lowest note for a flute is middle C and is one of the harder notes to produce.)

◆ 16. **Only a suggestion.** With very familiar hymns, you can hint at the melody, no more.

Example 2.29. "Holy, Holy, Holy," Tune: NICAEA, John Dykes, 1823–76.

◆ 17. **Toccata.** One of my favorites. Whoever invented the arpeggio was a genius. Rather than play block chords, play the notes down and then up again:

Example 2.30. Toccata figures.

Certainly one can look at Charles-Marie Widor's "Toccata" from the Fifth Symphony and see a mere F major chord (with a major 7th, E-natural added) arpeggiated down then up. (In Widor's "Toccata," the top of the arpeggio also mimics the theme played in the pedal later.) Try this arpeggiation with a hymn! Get the pattern going in the hands and forget about it and concentrate on the melody in the feet. This is especially helpful with instruments which don't have much bottom in the pedal. The best way to hear the melody in the feet, is to get the hands moving above!

Example 2.31. "Joy to the World," Tune: ANTIOCH, George F. Handel, 1685–1759.

Certainly, these suggestions are do-able by most people—some of them immediately, some of them next month. At any rate, with all the possibilities available, I hope you will agree that merely playing the first and last lines should be the last option.

HOW LONG SHOULD THE INTRODUCTION BE?

As long as it takes—as long as it takes to bring the body of singers into the spirit of the hymn. I have found that it takes longer to get people into quiet hymns than full hymns of praise. Sometimes it has taken me two or more times through the hymn "Silent Night" to get people quieted. I often keep it going until I hear the paper-rustling stop. Then it's amazing how the congregation thoughtfully and beautifully sings very quietly, rather than merely blatting out a familiar tune. For a full hymn like "Holy, Holy, Holy," a one or two measure introduction can be enough.

Where the hymn is placed in the service certainly is a major component to this question. The last hymn in an hour-and-a-half service should not have a long introduction. A hymn right after the sermon may be greatly enhanced by a longer introduction, allowing the thought process from the sermon to continue and merge with the hymn. The opening hymn may need a brief introduction, or may be helped by a full-length chorale prelude. In some traditions in Europe, the prelude to the service is an extended introduction to the opening hymn and then moves directly into the singing.

The most important point here is to be sensitive to what's going on in the service. How does the introduction and its length contribute to the flow of the service. What was before, and what follows? Does the introduction help, postpone or interrupt the flow?

IF THE PEOPLE COMPLAIN...

Our first reaction to complaints about free-introductions may be simply not to play them.

My hunch, however, is that the problem was not the introduction itself, but that the transition from introduction to singing was not clear, raising the DFA syndrome (Doubt, Fear, Abstinence). Rather than get caught dead singing the first phrase solo, people would tend to blame the introduction and tell you not to do "fancy" ones.

Check your transitions! Tape record them; try to sing the hymn; see if you are clear with your breathing.

Also consider *gradually* moving into doing free introductions. Perhaps one per month at first, then two per service. The church changeth like a turtle runneth.

Be patient. But be sure to be clear.

Chapter 3

STANZAS: For Heaven's Sake, Don't Be Dull!

...using the organ beyond piston 2

I once heard Dr. Walter Pelz joke about "piston 2." Piston 1 was, of course, for the prelude. Pistons 3-10 were naturally for the postlude. Everything in between was piston 2. All hymns and liturgies: piston 2. In my experience traveling around, and hearing such situations first hand, "piston 2" was usually a rather bland plenum. Not too loud, not too soft. I'm sure the intention was a sure-fire-no-anonymous-notes-in-the-offering-plate registration. Safe, but dull.

Whenever I hear such congregational song treatment, I wonder how it is that anyone would choose to attend services in that parish. Where there is little life, meaning is very difficult to notice. The people are blahed into a "muzak-stupor" that is neither exhuberant or meditative. It's just a gray blandness. It comes as no surprise to hear of congregations screaming for something else, or to hear of places that reduce the number of stanzas to the most-we-can-tolerate number. I can't blame them.

Unfortunately in these situations it is all too often the hymn itself that gets blamed, rather than the thoughtless treatment. Exchanging a hymn for some other music that is thought to be "lively" will not fix the blah syndrome felt earlier. You can't just replace dead flowers in the garden with new ones without stopping to notice that the first batch died because you didn't water them! The second batch will die too, if treated the same way.

On the other hand, in that which follows in this and the next chapter, I certainly hope you are not hearing me suggest that we create a dog-and-pony show with every hymn. For example, if the word "wings" appears, we release a flock of homing pigeons into the room. Or, as one friend of mine suggested, when the congregation sings "Rise, Shine, You People" we set many alarm clocks all around the room to go off simultaneously. She obviously was not serious, and something like that is not my intent.

There is such incredible variety in the texts set to music throughout any given service. Like any good symphony, good story, interesting landscape or sky full of clouds, there are ups and downs, peaks and valleys, highs and lows, fasts and slows. They're all there in the texts of the songs: from the prayerful plea for mercy of a *Kyrie,* to the picture of worship in heaven from the books of Isaiah and Revelation, to the Church on earth and the hosts of heaven rocking and shaking everything while singing, "Holy, holy, holy is the Lord Almighty; the whole earth is full of his glory."

Why on earth, then, would an organist use one bland sound for all of these? Why would there be one tempo? (One composition instructor once complained to the class, "What would we do without ♩ = 60?" It seems most of us were always using that tempo!) Why should there be a leveling of all of these texts musically into a flat nothingness?

WARNING! Blah accompaniment may be injurious to the imagery of the poetry, and may be the cause of thoughtlessness!

There are many ways in which the congregation's accompanist can help illuminate texts, to turn on the color: using other instruments with the hymns and liturgies, varying the tactus from song to song to match the nature of that which is being sung, varying the accompaniment to the tune in relation to the tune's origins, considering the tune's context in the service, and noting the text with which it has been paired.

But, the most obvious, and I think minimal demand, is to *vary the organ registration!*

ORCHESTRATE THE TEXT

As mentioned above, the nature of the texts can vary tremendously. This is true not only from hymn to hymn, but from stanza to stanza. Rarely in multiple stanza hymns does each stanza say exactly the same thing. How can the registration orchestrate the text?

First, two general points.

One, it is very important to include the full range of dynamic levels in the accompaniments. We need forte in order to have piano. Without pianissimo, we can't have fortissimo. The contrast must be present to have either. Make sure they are there.

And two, it is important to make use of the variety of colors available on the organ. This includes the sound of lush strings or no organ at all as the congregation sings a cappella. It includes Flutes alone and in various combinations, Principals and Reeds, and the gamut of pipe-lengths: 16′, 8′, 4′, 2′, 2 ⅔′, 1′, 1 ⅓′, 1 ⅗′. There are many varieties of color all itching to be exploited. No symphonic conductor would hire a full brass section and never use them. Nor would a composer/orchestrator use the entire orchestra for every phrase of a whole symphony. Sections rest. Various instruments and sections are put to use at just the right moment. There are peaks and valleys, climaxes and plateaus. Good orchestrators/composers make use of the available variety, knowing just when to apply the appropriate color. You need to find the appropriate moments to apply that wonderful 1′ Piccolo, or that moment when you push the tutti button during the *Sanctus.* It all comes from the texts. They tell all regarding orchestration.

CORE REGISTRATIONS FOR THE ORGAN

When deciding how to orchestrate a text, I think in terms of dynamic levels as a starting place, ranging from mezzo piano to forte. Naturally, I can go farther in either direction, and always do in fact, but for a practical level, let us begin with them.

Mezzo piano: Swell: Flute 8′, Flute 4′ (Maybe Flute 2′, if it is not too strong)
Great: Principals 8′ and 4′, Swell to Great coupler
Pedal: Subbass 16′ and 8′, Swell and Great to Pedal coupler

This is the minimum for beginning the singing. I think if you start with less, you raise the DFA syndrome (Doubt leading to Fear, Fear leading to Abstinence—in case you've jumped to this chapter and missed chapter 1). People may think you have a soloist in the bench you are going to pull out for the stanza if you start out with less than this. I have come to trust that an 8′and 4′ Principal combination is the sure cue for the people in the pews to sing. After the singing is going and established, the 4′ Principal can come off, as can even the 8′ Principal, and you can even come down to only the 8′ Flute of the Swell, or perhaps going all the way to accompanying with only the String and Celeste with the swell box closed for very still and quiet texts, as long as doubt does not surface in the pews. If it does, by all means, add more organ right away! It is possible that over time, a congregation can learn that it doesn't need much of a cue (if any!) and a mere breath is all that is needed. In that case one could start with less than the above "mezzo piano," but this is rare. The next levels would be (bracketed stops indicate stops added at each particular level):

Mezzo forte: Swell: Flutes 8′, 4′, 2′ [Principal 4′, perhaps Mixture]
Great: Principals 8′, 4′, [2′], Swell to Great
Pedal: Subbass 16′, 8′, [Principal 8′], Swell and Great to Pedal

Forte: Swell: Flutes 8′, 4′, 2′, Principal 4′, Mixture
Great: Principals 8′, 4′, [Mixture (turn off the 2′ Principal)][1], Swell to Great
Pedal: Principal 16′, [8′, 4′, Mixture], Swell and Great to Pedal

From there I would add the following stops in order:
Reed 8′ in the pedal
Reed 16′ in the pedal
Reed 8′ in the manual (usually in the Swell)
Reeds 16′, 4′ in the manuals (usually in the Swell)[2]
Any 32′ stops in the pedal (if you are so amazingly lucky to have them)
Remaining higher mixtures[3]

It is most often the case for me to have 6 pre-set sounds, piston 1 being Swell strings coupled to the Great with only an 8′ Flute on the Great. I use this for spots like the end of "Lamb of God," when we are singing "Grant us peace, grant us peace, grant us peace." Piston 2 would add an 8′ Principal from the Great to that, and perhaps a 4′ Flute. Piston 3 would be the mezzo piano described above, Piston 4, mezzo forte above, Piston 5, forte, and Piston 6 adding the Reeds to the Pedal and Swell. And these are mere "core" sounds that I vary as I go by manually adding and deleting stops.

On three-manual instruments, most often the third division is not needed for the "ensemble" for congregational singing. This division is often called the "Positiv," coming from the German tradition of "Rück-Positiv," a small-scale division hanging on the balcony rail behind the key desk. These divisions are best for gently soloing a melody close to the congregation with a "cornet"

---

[1]Care must be given here. In most instruments, the mixture of the Great includes a 2′ Principal. If you leave the 2′ Principal on, and add the Mixture to it, the two separate 2′ Principal ranks can argue with each other and cause quite the sound in hearing aids.

[2]Sometimes I have accomplished this on instruments with only an 8′ Trumpet on the Swell by using the Swell to Great 16′, 8′ and 4′ together. If I do this, I must be sure to turn off the 8′ Flutes on the Swell, so I don't create muck!

[3]Sometimes I have had to accomplish this with the use of super couplers like Swell to Great 4′, or Great to Great 4′. BE CAREFUL that this doesn't create more acoustical argument than excitement!

sound (Flutes 8′, 4′, 2′, $2\frac{2}{3}'$, and $1\frac{3}{5}'$), accompanied with Principal 8′ on the Great. This is wonderful for small gatherings. At some churches this division is called the "Choir" division and resembles a second Swell division. These often are designed to do as the name suggests: accompany the choir, not necessarily the congregation.

In my current situation, I have available on the Positiv manual a wonderful festival trumpet stop which can carry a tune over a full sound on the Great. In all of my presets, I have this trumpet available all the time, ready for any moment that my right hand gets itchy to solo out the melody. In fuller sounds, I use it at the 16′ *and* 8′ octaves to carry over a fortissimo chorus on the Great. This is my favorite use of horizontal trumpets in congregational singing. Unfortunately, most horizontal trumpets are only available on the Great (often technically necessary from an organ building standpoint), and therefore can't be used to bring a melody out over the full chorus of the Great division.

A good rule of thumb for chorus registrations would be: if you can't hear it come on as you add it to the chorus, don't use it. It's only more for you to keep track of. Strive for adding higher and/or lower octaves before duplicating an octave. For example: I would add a 4′ Flute to an 8′ Principal before I would add another 8′ Flute to it. Loading up on 8′ stops (the same pitch level of the congregation's voice) doesn't add as much as higher and lower octaves unless you are after a warmer sound. Think of expanding in both directions: higher and lower as you build the sound.

So, how does one decide what sound to use? The text tells all. Let's put one through the process.

SAMPLE APPLICATION

All Creatures of Our God and King

1 All creatures of our God and King,
Lift up your voice with us and sing:
Alleluia, Alleluia!
O burning sun with golden beam
And silver moon with softer gleam:
Oh praise him! Oh, praise him!
Alleluia, Alleluia, Alleluia!

2 O rushing wind and breezes soft
O clouds that ride the winds aloft:
Oh, praise him! Alleluia!
O rising morn, in praise rejoice
O lights of evening, find a voice
Oh, praise him! Oh, praise him!
Alleluia, Alleluia, Alleluia!

3 O flowing waters, pure and clear,
Make music for your Lord to hear.
Oh, praise him! Alleluia!
O fire so masterful and bright,
Providing us with warmth and light,
Oh, praise him! Oh, praise him!
Alleluia, alleluia, alleluia!

4 Dear mother earth, who day by day
Unfolds rich blessings on our way,
Oh, praise him! Alleluia!
The fruits and flow'rs that verdant grow,
Let them his praise abundant show.
Oh, praise him! Oh, praise him!
Alleluia, alleluia, alleluia!

5 O ev'ryone of tender heart.
Forgiving others, take your part,
Oh, praise him! Alleluia!
All you who pain and sorrow bear,
Praise God and lay on him your care.
Oh, praise him! Oh, praise him!
Alleluia, alleluia, alleluia!

6 And you, most kind and gentle death,
Waiting to hush our final breath
Oh, praise him! Oh, praise him!
You lead to heav'n this child of God,
Where Christ our Lord the way has trod.
Oh, praise him! Oh, praise him!
Alleluia, alleluia, alleluia!

7 Let all things their Creator bless
And worship God in humbleness.
Oh, praise him! Alleluia!
Oh, praise the Father, praise the Son,
And praise the Spirit, Three in One,
Oh, praise him! Oh, praise him!
Alleluia, Alleluia, Alleluia!

Text: Francis of Assisi, 1182–1226; tr. William H. Draper, 1855–1933, alt.

I can imagine that the reaction to seven stanzas is often a "GASP! Which of these are we going to cut?" I'll comment on that practice in a moment. But if we creatively orchestrate all seven stanzas, it shouldn't feel like such a chore to get through them all. They are each and every one wonderful images, and quite different! If we accompany them all the same, we deny this wonderful poetry its full richness.

Let's assign a level to each stanza.

One: Full sound, perhaps fortissimo (full to Mixture, with 8′ Reed on manuals, 16′ and 8′ Reeds on pedal). It says unapologetically "All Creatures," not just a few of them—ALL CREATURES. Give the people permission to sing out on this stanza with fullness!

Two: "Breezes soft", "Rushing wind." This is a quieter image than stanza one. This needs to come down in fullness, I would say, to the "mezzo piano" previously described. Perhaps add the Swell Mixture for the refrain.

Three: "Flowing Waters." Even quieter. After the stanza is rolling, I would remove any 2′ stops, and the 4′ Principals, getting down to a smooth and gentle sound.

Four: This stanza's imagery doesn't say full or gentle to me, it simply is. I would go back to either a mezzo forte or forte for this stanza for the sake of contrast.

Five: "Tender heart," "pain and sorrow bear." Certainly not loud. Perhaps mezzo piano to piano—again, quite a contrast from stanza 4.

Six: "Kind and gentle death." For this stanza, how about using the one stop absolutely every organ has: NO STOP! Let the congregation sing it without accompaniment. I would begin with piano sound, then little by little remove stops—first higher octaves, then principals, then flutes, then quit playing the soprano line, the alto line, the tenor, and finally the bass—all the time listening to be sure the DFA syndrome has not arisen. It's also good to disappear on a weak beat so the breath is not dependent on the organ's continuing. If you are gone before the people arrive at a breath, they will deal with the breath on their own.

Interlude? Perhaps. With this many stanzas, if all have sung 1–6, it might be a good re-energizer. With interludes and modulating up a half step, I would try not falling into the cliché which dictates that both always preceed the last stanza, regardless of the text. I do interludes far more frequently than modulating. In fact I seldom modulate. But how about interludes after stanza 1, or 3, or other places rather than only before the last stanza? If stanza six of this hymn is sung unaccompanied, the absence of an interlude may be more dramatic than an interlude.

Seven: Coming out of an a cappella stanza, you wouldn't need much registration for it to feel like great guns! I would begin with forte, or mezzo-forte, and build to full organ by the end of the stanza, adding as each new phrase begins. (A new setting would also be effective, but that's coming up in subsequent chapters!)

There! Seven stanzas, and hardly two are alike! In fact, from a "loudness" standpoint, there are only two (perhaps three) out of seven that would be forte or more. Most are quieter! This is more effective than merely reading the title and playing all stanzas accordingly.

This process should be gone through for everything the congregation sings—liturgies, hymns (all stanzas), and psalms—all of these! The *Kyrie* and *Lamb of God* should be quite different from *Glory to God*, or *Holy, Holy, Holy*. Read the words. They tell you which registrations of the organ to use.

I hope, if nothing else, you feel a twinge of guilt if you thoughtlessly play through congregational songs without at least thinking about what they mean. Thoughtful hymn preparation is a lot of work, but, I maintain, FAR more important than that which many organists spend most of their preparations doing—the POP (prelude, offertory, postlude). It is in the congregational song that vibrancy is unleashed. It is here that a visitor will notice as Eric Routly said regarding choir, but the same could be said about congregational song accompanied by the organ. "When your choir sings, you should hope that people coming into your church will say, not, 'What a good choir they've got,' but 'What a good God they've got.'"[4]

A brief word about eliminating stanzas. My grandmother passed away several years ago. Her death was not a fast one. She literally went limb by limb. A stroke would leave an arm limp. Her sense of balance went, so her legs no longer could hold her body erect. She was ready to go. We were ready to let her go. At her funeral, we sang the text studied above: "All Creatures of Our God and King." I no longer sing stanza 6 without thinking of her. "And you most kind and gentle death, waiting to hush our final breath. Alleluia. You lead to heaven the child of God, where Christ the Lord our way has trod." Powerful. We don't know the stories that our worshipers bring to the hymns that we sing. Who are we to say we do not have time for this meaning?

That is not to say that there may not be situations for which careful thought and thematic thrust may lead to selecting stanzas and excluding others. This, I feel would be rare.

While many of our hymns are translations, and have already eliminated stanzas, the poetry of most hymns is a complete journey that becomes disjointed when portions are eliminated. Can you imagine an announcement: "We will only be confessing the first and third articles of the Apostles' Creed today?" Such is the flow of many hymns. One must be careful.

Rather, if the accompanist and music planners do their job right, things are varied and interesting enough that the 30 seconds saved by eliminating a stanza is not even considered.

---

[4]Erik Routley: *Music Leadership in the Church* (New York, Nashville: Abingdon Press, 1967), p. 97.

WORKING WITH LESS-THAN-DESIRED INSTRUMENTS

How few of us really have the instrument we would like! My father always says that we organists are the pickiest bunch there is. There is always something not right with the instruments we are provided with. "If I only had that 32′ Reed." Some of you say, "If I only had any Reed or a Mixture!" I've played on a variety of "things" ranging from a one manual split keyboard (very small) organ, to a 13-rank North German "squealer" (built on a 4′ Principal, that's right—no 8′ Principal), a 1920's "mush-box," electronic organs, to the very nice 54-rank Reuter that Paul Manz helped design that I currently play. I love this one. (Except, it doesn't have a 32′ Reed!)

Each instrument provides challenges, yet all are still capable of variety. Here are some tips for some typical situations:

Old-electronic organs

Use as few stops as possible. Most of the stops are probably generated from the same electronic tone foundation and sent out through the same speaker. Different stops do very little other than alter the electronic over-tones. Find one stop from each octave level to get the clearest sound. I usually find the best clarity in the flutes. Avoid loading up on the 8′ stops for more sound.

Newer electronic instruments are doing a much better job of variety in tone production, even to dramatically increasing the number of speakers and tone generators to imitate the "chorus" effect. Tonal design is also improving greatly.

No-guts "Squealers"

It was in playing these that I learned the art of double pedal. Most of the time the strongest sound below 8′ was a hooty 16′ Subbass. I discovered that I could play both feet in octaves for a little more sound, or with ending chords play an open fifth with my feet to create a "resultant" 32′ effect, albeit false. I sometimes used the 4′ Principal on the manual while playing down an octave for a thicker 8′ sound. For a "celeste," even though I had no string on the instrument, I would couple the two 8′ Flutes together. It was a warmer sound that worked. For ending chords, I would double down (or up) an octave with my hands to get more sound. I exploited every stop as much as possible—playing the 2′ Flute down an octave for yet another 4′ Flute sound.

Early 20th century "Mush-box"

This instrument was unified all over the place, and I had to break every "rule" in the book to get more of a variety of sound. Instruments of this era included super octave couplers. I used them! I did have a 2 $\frac{2}{3}$′ Quinte (Principal) on the Great, which together with the 2′ stop and the Great to Great 4′, provided a quasi 4-rank Mixture. Often I would put the Great to Great 16′ and 4′, and the Swell to Great 16′, 8′, and 4′, and play up an octave. This provided a much fuller sound. The one bleak reed available on the Swell was frequently coupled down at different octaves for variety of color. With these instruments, like old electronic instruments, the fewer 8′ stops you use the clearer it will be. Purists and organ builders will shudder and write bad reviews of this book after reading this paragraph, but I have to say it is better to follow the intent of the rules and create interest rather than the legalism of the rules and get boredom. Even if one loses some clarity, baroque counterpoint was not at issue. And besides, there wasn't much clarity to begin with in that organ.

Ideally, an excellent instrument has no need of unification (using one rank of pipes for many stops). The ranks designed into the instrument are complete enough not to need some of the above tricks. If the right combinations of various octaves are included, super couplers are not needed. An additional bright Mixture added to the Swell or Positiv will help keep things clearer than adding a Swell to Great 4′. But sometimes these things just aren't possible or existent, and we have to resort to getting the best sound however possible.

WORKING WITH THE LESS-THAN-IDEAL NUMBER OF WORSHIPERS

Naturally we would like all of our worship spaces to be full all the time, certainly every time we include singing. And how many times have we set the pistons with this ideal in mind, to find that as we finish the prelude, we look out to see a handful of die-hards out there because the Super Bowl started a half-hour before worship. Your mind rushes immediately to the certain anonymous notes you are going to get if you still use the forte you have set up for the entrance hymn, "Praise to the Lord."

What do you do with hymns that call for fullness? If you tone down and only use mezzo piano, the congregation will sing that way. If you use your regular forte you will blow them out of the room! HELP!

It is tricky dealing with smaller groups: funerals, weddings, or regular services when you aren't going to get a full house in attendance. Somehow you need to create a full sound that doesn't blow people out of the water, but enough that gives those who are there permission to sing full praise when called for.

You might consider building your fortes starting with the 8′ Principal, and gradually adding flutes and oboes instead of more and higher principals and trumpets. Use only a lighter mixture, or only a 2′ stop. For forte, complete with reed, omit the Mixture and close the box. For stanzas that aren't obviously full praise, use Principals 8′ and 4′, and solo out the melody with a Cornet or 8′ Trumpet. The trick is not to play so quietly that doubt rises (people will be afraid to sing out), and yet still give a feel of fullness that allows them to sing out even in a sparse situation, but doesn't out-do those present. Moving to the Swell box and perhaps closing the box to tone things down a bit creates a problem: it is not enough foundation to be a sure cue for those who ARE there to sing out since most Swell divisions do not include an 8′ Principal. Finding the best sound for this situation is not an easy task, but one worth exploring for a solution. Perhaps this is the greatest advantage to the multi-level solid state systems available today: Bank A has 10 generals for a full house; Bank B for 1/2 full house, Bank C for a "measle-peep" gathering, etc.

"THE ORGAN IS TOO LOUD!"

Have you heard this? I have. Still do. If you do all that I have said in this chapter, you will. Here are some things to think about when you hear it:

◆ 1. The criticism may be right. Recheck your settings. Are they too much for the people? Can you hear the congregation's voice with the organ? Pare the organ down a bit. Especially check your use of mixtures together with other higher pitch stops such as 2′ or 1′. Remove the 4′ Reed, or the 1 $\frac{1}{3}$′ stop.

◆ 2. Discuss the reasons with those who complain. Did they notice the text when the organ got "fuller"? (It might be good to avoid the word "loud.") There was a reason you added the trumpet. (Be sure you thought about it when doing it so that this moment can go smoothly.)

◆ 3. Remember that you play assuming that the people are singing. If they are not singing, of course it will sound loud. If I know people who complain had not been singing, I politely listen to their concern and thank them for sharing it. But for the sake of those for whom the accompaniment to singing is meaningful, I don't act on the complaint.

◆ 4. Could it be a planning problem? Are all the selected hymns mighty hymns of praise? It is better to select a variety of hymns requiring contrasting dynamic levels.

◆ 5. Where were people sitting? Some people simply don't like anything louder than a soft breeze. Different parts of the room may be quieter.

◆ 6. It could be the organ, not you! If it is too loud for the singing, it may not have been designed properly. It could be that the organ needs to be re-voiced or even re-designed. Make it your service/repair person's problem. I once asked Paul Manz if he used the whole organ often with congregational singing, to which he replied, "Why not?" That really stayed with me. If the congregation has spent thousands and thousands of dollars on an instrument, why not use it? It would be good stewardship. Have it revoiced: re-design it so that you can use it. It's worth the expense! (Usually it's the other way around—the organ is too small! As Paul Manz said on another occasion, "It's like a Volkswagon Beetle engine trying to pull a Greyhound bus full of people up a mountain.")

◆ 7. Get rid of the carpeting or pew pads. They may be accentuating the bad and squelching the good (i.e., the people's voices).

◆ 8. Remember the prophetic nature of your work. If people have only been used to "measle-peep" accompaniments, give them time to notice that there is a reason why it is accompanied with a "full" sound. Be patient. Reevaluate.

We're off to a good start. You could stop here, and I would feel good about our progress together. I'm convinced that if we did a more interesting job with just breathing, tactus, the introductions and registration, the first question may not be, "Where is the contemporary service?!"

But there's more....

Chapter 4

STANZAS: More Possibilities!

...variety beyond the accompaniment itself

Remembering that a good number of parishioners normally do not sing anywhere other than at church and perhaps in the shower, I believe that we can do even more with the hymnody than everyone singing all of the stanzas exactly the same way. We can do more than I have outlined so far with accompaniment and introductions in encouraging the people to maintain a strong sense of vitality throughout the whole hymn. Vitality doesn't necessarily mean full and strong singing. It means that the people remain in touch with the meaning of the song and remain participatory throughout the whole song rather than thinking about the meal they've got in the oven when they notice that after singing three stanzas, there are four to go!

I can remember from studying service playing in Germany, the typical hymn had eight to ten stanzas. Many of them had more. Imagine if the German chorales in our current hymnals included all of the original stanzas! John, the person who sits at a security desk all night long, would probably move from thoughts about lunch on to what to serve for dinner, and perhaps on to planning next month's family budget before you get to stanza eight.

Preparing the use of the organ, and preparing an effective introduction as described in the previous chapters will help. But if a hymn has more than three stanzas, and your acoustics are dry as a bedroom, seven, six, five or even four stanzas can be a lot.

And what about Jane, who teaches voice all week. She is not only eager to sing all the stanzas, she's interested in the alto part, much to the annoyance of the person sitting next to her. That person can't read a note of music and can't figure out what hymn Jane is singing because it surely doesn't sound like the melody to the hymn we're all supposed to be singing.

Multiple stanzas encourage the use of multiple levels of singers. It seems natural to me why so many cultures have practiced dialogical singing. Dialogical singing means that people take turns—as if to have a conversation in song—a conversation with God and with each other. It could be between a leader and an assembly, choir and assembly, right and left sides of the assembly, whatever can be imagined. It could involve antiphonal singing—two groups or leader and group singing a continually changing text. Or it could involve responsorial singing—when the people sing the same refrain, and the verses are sung by a choir or leader. Psalm singing is often antiphonal, by half-verse or by whole verse. African music is often dialogical between leader and people. It would seem unfortunate to me if the congregation's singing is entirely responsorial. As one acquaintance put it, "then all our people will be on their deathbeds and only know refrains!"

Singing texts in their entirety is important as it becomes a part of our memory, a deeper part of ourselves that at some point we will need to draw upon.

DIALOGICAL DIMENSIONS TO CONGREGATIONAL SINGING

In jazz groups, a simple blues pattern of three chords can be effectively extended to last quite a while. But if everyone played exactly the same thing each time through the pattern, how dull it would be. The players take turns. The trumpet player gets up and "takes one," a solo verse while the remaining players slip into accompaniment mode, listening as the trumpeter explores how many different sounds he/she can squeal out of the instrument and harmonies from that pattern. When someone takes a solo verse it does not mean that the remaining players are no longer participating. In fact they are most likely keenly tuned into what the solo player is doing because they can learn some new licks, or will want to support a rhythmic motive that the player may be improvising. The group also simply goes with whatever instruments are there. A leader will look around the group and point: "you take the next one." All players do their part and know when to allow someone else to do the same.

Our congregational hymns and songs can do similar things, not just with instrumentalists, but with singers. When there are ten stanzas, we can pass some of them around to various singers. John can take the back seat while the women sing one stanza, and he can follow the text. Some of the stanzas can be in harmony, so that people like Jane can boldly do the alto line. The choir, who has the advantage of this thing called "the rehearsal," can learn a different setting for stanza five. The flute player can prepare something to render stanza six. Your eighth grade soloist, who loves to sing, can sing stanza two.

This age-old practice of alternation is not a practice of exclusion, but of further inclusion. It allows musicians to plug into the hymns in ways relative to their ability; it allows rests for persons who don't sing a lot in their lives; and it gives more energy for the stanzas they do sing. Ask a trumpet player if it would be wise to play a symphony where the trumpet plays in every measure. Rest energizes the nonrest.

It always amazes me after having some octave-specific stanzas (such as men and women) how much the singing increases when all come back together in song. Maybe because the family is all looking at DAD during the "men's" stanza to be sure he's singing. When all sing again, DAD is relieved to be off the hook and sings out of joy in having company!

In addition to providing rests, practicing alternation is another form of variety in orchestration. In Chapter 3. I discuss how orchestration can help illuminate the meaning of the text. Alternation of voices as discussed here is yet another way to do just that. Like a good symphony that uses a variety of colors (not the same sound throughout), practicing alternation helps hymns be more interesting. Study a Mozart score, noticing the alternation between strings and winds. Not at all monotonous.

OPTIONS—SUGGESTIONS—EXAMPLES

A list of alternation possibilities

Workshop attendees love handouts. Especially when there is a numbered list. Here's one for alternation possibilities. Consider this list the beginning of yours, adding to it over the years.

- ◆ 1. **Alternate octaves.** I use the terms men/women. It's not a gender thing; it's a vocal octave thing for the most part. Children are indeed included—the boys kind of like being identified with the men, girls with the women. When I see "women and children" to identify the upper octave, I don't imagine the 12-year-old boy responding to that well! The terms "high and low" voices can (and for me has) confused people. Are altos low voices? Are tenors high voices? I find "men and women" to be the clearest.

This practice could be used from stanza to stanza, or even within a stanza. Consider the hymn "Lord, Thee I Love with All My Heart." Women could begin stanza 2 with the men joining them at "Lord Jesus Christ..." This instills some new energy for this last section of that hymn. Then for stanza 3, the reverse could happen: men could begin, women joining at the same spot. Hymns with refrains seem to invite everyone to join in again at the refrain, but refrains don't always have to be so. The important thing is that people know easily (and can remember) when they are to sing.

◆ 2. **Alternate harmony and unison.** This too could be from stanza to stanza, or within a stanza. The "alleluias" of "All Creatures of Our God and King" during stanza 4 could be sung in harmony, the rest in unison. Some traditions sing as a rule in harmony, and in this case it would be good to suggest an occasional unison stanza.

I think of singing in harmony as an option to do once in a while, depending on the community. In my parishes I generally suggest that the first and last stanzas be sung by everyone in unison. This is to be sure that the person who does not read music, who will naturally be drawn to the melody, will have as much help as possible. I also strive not to do the same thing twice in a row, unless the people can't help it. Harmony is wonderful, and in some traditions the norm, but I treat it as one of the many options and do not use it too many times in a row—again, for the sake of those who sing primarily melody. If we pull all the music readers off the melody and onto the parts, the nonreaders do not have the advantage of their help. But there does need to be opportunity for part-singing, and, if there are those who love to do it, it needs to be blessed!

◆ 3. **Soloist and congregation.** Imagine a 2nd grade child singing stanza 1 of "Your Little Ones Dear Lord, Are We" or as in the British tradition, stanza 1 of "Once in Royal David's City." Stanzas 1–5 of "From Heaven Above" are the words of an angel: how about a soloist? The congregation can begin singing at stanza 6 "How glad we'll be to find it so!..." Or, for stanzas 2 and 3 of "All Creatures of Our God and King," have soloists sing the text, inviting the congregation to join for the word "Alleluia." This really brings out the "rushing wind and breezes soft." Alternate phrase by phrase with two different soloists for even more dialogical effect. Or consider using more than one soloist, in different parts of the room. This is not a new idea: the "Quempas Carol" did this, phrase by phrase, in different corners of the room. Imagine having a stanza of "In Christ There Is No East or West" making use of this practice!

◆ 4. **Use the choir.** This section is especially useful for the SMALL CHOIR (2 or more people). Assign some stanzas to the choir, and unleash the myriad of possibilities, since they have the big "R" (rehearsal). Here are some ideas:

a. **Unison.** Just sing a stanza in unison, without accompaniment. This works especially well with children, but also with adults.

b. **Men and women.** Alternate men and women within a stanza intended for the choir. In stanza 3 of "A Hymn of Glory Let Us Sing," have the sections in quotes sung by women, the narrative spots sung by men. Have both sing "Alleluia," perhaps even in harmony.

Example 4.1. "A Hymn of Glory Let Us Sing," Stanza 3, Text: The Venerable Bede, 673–735; tr. Hymnal Version, 1978. © 1978, *Lutheran Book of Worship*. Tune: LASST UNS ERFREUEN, *Geistliche Kirchengesänge*, Köln, 1623.

c. **Alternating texture.** Alternate unison and harmony if the structure of the text and melody seem to allow it. Examine the text to determine where harmony compliments the text and where unison emphasizes the text.

Example 4.2. "A Mighty Fortress Is Our God," Tune: EIN FESTE BURG, Martin Luther, 1483–1546.

d. **Four parts.** Of course, the choir can just sing the 4-part setting provided in the hymnal, if it is indeed a vocal 4-voice setting.

e. **Canon.** Either by octaves (soprano/alto, and tenor/bass), sections, or in equal voices. Experiment. Try "Let All Mortal Flesh" in canon just as chapter 2 did for the organist. Pentatonic hymns such as "Jerusalem, My Happy Home," or many of the other early American hymns work especially well in canon, but many more do as well. Find out if any given hymn works in canon by trying it! Also consider having more than four-part canons! Six or eight or even more! Experiment, and remember that it need not always be "pretty." Try stanza 3 of "A Mighty Fortress" in 3-part canon at the half-measure up to the last phrase. It will not be pretty, but the words "one little word subdues him" will leap off the page. Perhaps have only one person sing that last line instead of the whole choir.

f. **Ostinato.** Have a part of the choir sing a continuous pattern, and another section the tune for any given stanza. For example:

Ex. 4.3. "Lord, Whose Love in Humble Service," stanza 2, Text: Albert F. Bayly, 1901–84. © 1988 Oxford University Press. Tune: BEACH SPRING, *The Sacred Harp*, Philadelphia, 1844. Arrangement: © Nancy Maeker. Used by permission.

Or, give a four-part ostinato to a small group, while most of the rest of the choir sings the melody and text:

Example 4.4. "O Morning Star, How Fair and Bright," stanza 5, Text and tune: Philipp Nicolai, 1556–1608. Tr. hymnal version, 1978. Text © *Lutheran Book of Worship,* Arrangement: David M. Cherwien.

Try this with some other hymns. Again, early American hymns or hymns that are primarily pentatonic work especially well with this technique.

g. **Two parts.** Write out a simple two-part setting, where one part sings the melody, the other something free. Exchange the 2-voices for the second phrase.

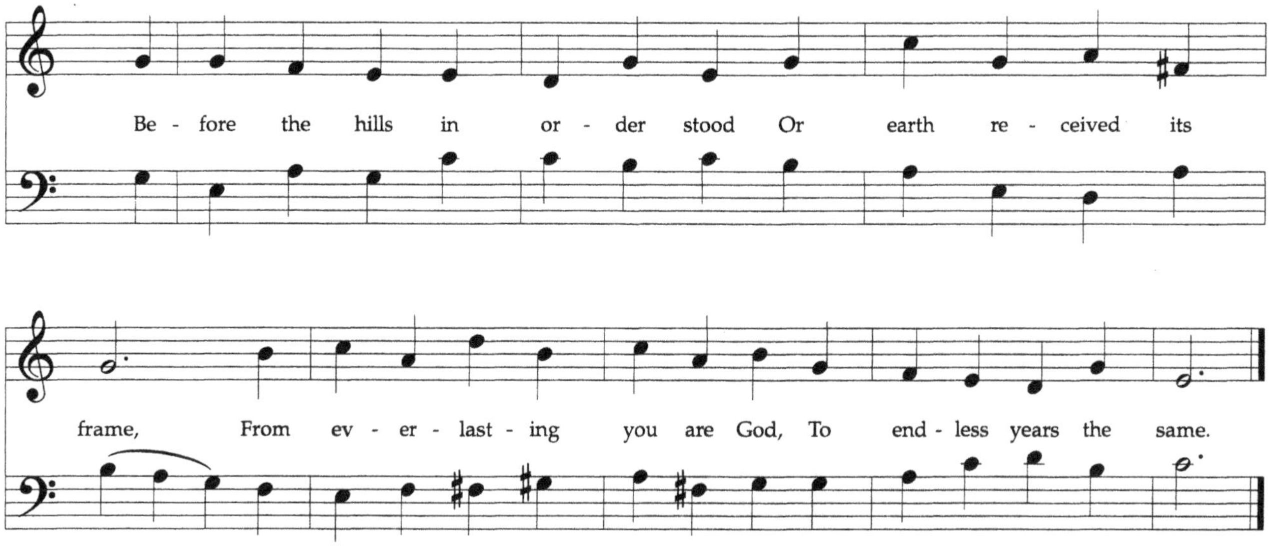

Example 4.5. "O God Our Help in Ages Past," stanza 3, Text: Isaac Watts, 1674–1748. Tune: William Croft, 1678–1727.

h. **Chorale preludes and voices.** Use a chorale prelude, having the choir sing the melody instead of soloing it out on the organ. A great example would be J. S. Bach's "Wachet auf." Be careful about the key. Be sure the arrangement is in the same key as the hymnal.[1] This could work with many of the current publications of hymn related materials for organ. In the example below, the meter even changes:

[1]Let me tell you by experience: the service itself is not the time to finally practice going from the Bach setting to the hymnal, only to find they are in two different keys!

Example 4.6. "Songs of Thankfulness and Praise," Text: Christopher Wordsworth, 1807-85. Tune: SALZBURG, Christopher Anton, d. 1658. Organ setting: David M. Cherwien, *Interpretations, Book IX,* © 1992, Summa Productions, Minneapolis, MN 55414-1510.

Another caution: I would accomplish this type of variation by cueing the choir instead of writing it out, as in many cases you may be violating copyright laws for rearranging copyrighted publications. This also saves paper.

i. **Instant descant.** Have the sopranos and tenors sing the alto line up an octave for an immediate descant. Try this on stanza 2, rather than only on the last stanza.

j. **Up an octave.** Sopranos and tenors sing up an octave in appropriate spots, such as the last "Alleluia" of "In Thee Is Gladness," or "Now All the Vault of Heaven Resounds," or many of the hymns that end in the lower end of the scale. This adds energy to the end of a hymn.

k. **Published literature.** Purchase some choir arrangements of stanzas, or extract a special choral setting of a particular stanza from a hymn concertato without using the entire setting for all stanzas. (More about concertato settings later).

l. **A soloist.** Alternate soloist and full choir, or have the choir hum the harmony as a soloist sings the melody and text.

◆ 5. **A single instrument.** Use an instrument for a stanza by itself, with the congregation reading the text. Or use an organ setting, giving the melody of the hymn to an instrument instead of a solo stop on the organ.

◆ 6. **Organ alone.** Have the organ "sing" the text of a particular stanza as the congregation reads the words. This can be improvised, or make use of the many, many compositions for organ based on hymns. Be sure the arrangement does indeed reflect the text and not the abilities of the organist. And don't merely use a clever arrangement.

◆ 7. **Highlighting a different voice.** Use an instrument on the alto or tenor line as the congregation sings.

Perhaps by now your own ideas are beginning to jump into your mind. As you can see, the possibilities are tremendous. We are limited only by our fear and the lack of energy put into the congregation's song.

A very important point is that the musician (or person charged with the responsibility of implementing the congregation's song) must *know the people*—what their particular resources and capabilities are, and what possibilities the space provides. Then exploit the possibilities! If you have choirs, plug them into the hymnody! If you have instrumentalists, plug them in here as well! If you have two balconies, do something with them! If you have soloists, use them. If you have a large number of men who read music, give them a stanza, encouraging them to improvise harmony, à-la-barbershop!

IT'S NOT A LARGE-CHURCH THING!

For those of you in smaller church situations, I have experienced this practice extremely helpful—perhaps even more so than in large situations. For example, how difficult it is in large churches for a junior high flute student even to get all the way up the mountain of bureaucracy to the holy musician's office, not to mention the audition fright! In small parishes, with limited musical resources, perhaps one stanza of "Have No Fear, Little Flock" played by that young flutist as the introduction to the hymn would be more accessible than a Telemann sonata for the prelude. Or perhaps a soloist could sing a stanza of a hymn rather than Malotte's "The Lord's Prayer." Soloists and instrumentalists can be especially helpful in a church where there is no choir.

In fact, the things that I have covered so far in the entire book: hymn introductions, organ registration, color, alternation possibilities, all have **nothing** to do with the size of the congregation.

GENERAL CAUTIONS

Moderation is a very important word to remember. If people are not used to all of this creativity, doing too much too quickly may disengage rather than engage. Perhaps do something creative once a month with one of the hymns. Next year do it twice a month. Then perhaps only on the hymn of the day. From there gradually increase.

Second, remember to BE CLEAR about ***who*** sings and ***when*** they are to sing.

WARNING! Excessive monkey shines may lead to loss of support and participation, and may be injurious to your employment!

The bulletin is the most likely place to assign creative alternation. It needs to be clear. People need to know when to sing. If they begin singing a stanza assigned to someone else they may be embarrassed. Remember that the people need to glance quickly at the bulletin during a hymn and easily find the stanza instructions to see if they sing the next stanza. Here are two examples for "Joy to the World" with its surrounding bulletin items:

Good

page 56	**CONFESSION and FORGIVENESS**
Hymn 39	**ENTRANCE HYMN**: "Joy to the World"
	Stanza 1: All
	Stanza 2: Women
	Stanza 3: Men
	Stanza 4: All
page 57	**GREETING**
page 57	**KYRIE** (etc.)

Bad

Brief Order for Confession and Forgiveness–page 56

Entrance Hymn 39 "Joy to the World"

Stanza 1 all, 2 women, 3 men, 4 all

Greeting—page 57

Kyrie—page 57, etc.

The second example may look OK to the typist, but remember that the men are going to have to quickly find the instructions for stanza three during the end of stanza two. In the second example that's not easy to find. Be clear. If you aren't, you may be asked not to do alternations any more, which could lead to stanza slashing. ("We're only going to sing stanzas one and four.") Most complaints about alternation are related to finding the instructions, which is related to the DFA syndrome![2]

[2]DFA Syndrome: Doubt, which leads to Fear, which leads to Abstinence. See chapter 1.

In some situations, who does which stanza could be spontaneously decided by the worshipers themselves. I have this vision that I carry with me from the rock-band days: every time we performed a song, it was never the same twice, partly due to the improvisatory nature of rock music. We were always listening to each other, getting ideas from each other, giving each other hints. If a harmony note was missing in the vocals, someone would jump to it. I believe congregational song can indeed carry this spontaneity! I can imagine the people themselves deciding as they go that this stanza is in harmony. One person starts singing parts, and the others join quickly. One stanza the people leave for the women, the next for the men. Descants or improvised harmony (such as in Africa) erupt naturally from the pews! It can indeed happen. I have experienced it in parishes and experience it in my own parish—especially harmony. It's exciting to hear harmony start and then spread throughout the room. If it is going really well, I often drop out and really highlight it! The choir knows that if one particular stanza is sung in harmony, the next will be in unison, unless they absolutely can't help it, such as in "Children of the Heavenly Father." I would not hit them over the head with an alternative harmonization in an attempt to get a power struggle going (unless the DFA syndrome arises). I let them have at it!

THE NEW HYMN

There may also be another reason for alternation. If a particular hymn is brand new to a congregation, it would be extremely helpful for the choir (or soloist) to sing stanza 1. The congregation then sings stanza 2. The choir or soloist then sings stanza 3 (so the congregation can hear how stanza 2 was to have gone). By stanza 4 they have it down. This is a very helpful way to "teach" new hymns—by actually doing them in nonthreatening ways.

THE HYMN CONCERTATO

This may be a term unknown to you. Publishers in the past years have been producing hymn concertatos by the dozens! They are entire hymns: all stanzas, written with introductions, stanza alternations composed into the setting, alternative harmonizations, choir stanzas, descants, and "optional" instruments. An organist can buy a full score and use it for the introductions and alternative harmonizations. The choir uses octavo scores for choir stanzas. The congregation simply sings out of the hymnal. In some cases, that particular hymn may not be in the hymnal, but the publisher will provide a reproducible "congregational page." All creative components are prescribed for you.

However, if you do everything I describe herein, and learn to improvise as I am espousing, you will not need to buy these.

THAT'S RIGHT—ALL THE STANZAS

I believe if we work harder on variety, both in hymn selection, placement in the service, and in practice, each hymn becomes a looked-forward-to journey that begins with the first note of the introduction and continues to the end of the last stanza. Eliminating stanzas may leave people feeling cheated! Upon occasion, thematically it makes sense to eliminate a stanza about celebrating the Eucharist if a hymn is being sung in a non-Eucharist service.

We've triggered the creative juices. Now what about the "I" word (Improvisation) for the accompanist?

Read on!

Chapter 5

ACCOMPANIMENT:

Moving Beyond Hymnal Settings

Somewhere along the course of North American history, accompanists developed this unspoken law: all hymns must be accompanied by organ (including using the old electronic organ Joe gave the church when he got a new one for his home), using homophonic four-part settings printed in the hymnal. To violate this law is to be too radical and confusing for the common no-mind in the pew.

Certainly we do not wish to do things that will confuse the singers: the accompaniment's purpose after all is to help people sing, not to show how clever the accompanist is.

However, there can be much more to life than a four-part setting.

> **WARNING! Being creative with the accompaniment may increase interest and delight in congregational song, and may increase your workload!**

ROCK AND JAZZ PRINCIPLE

Coupling my experience at a hymn festival led by Paul Manz with my experience in the rock band, I learned that congregational hymns can be enlivened with more freedom than we think, without confusing the singers.

The unspoken principle we operated with in the band was this: the melody and words were the given. What we did around and under them was totally up for grabs! The options ranged from what the instrumentation was, to the harmonies and even rhythmic and melodic counterpoint. We were always in search of a more interesting chord or counterrhythm for any given spot. We had tremendous freedom and helped the songs become unique again each time we did them.

Why not with the church's song? Certainly when the congregation is singing in four parts, the accompanist will need to play the hymnal setting, or at least the setting being sung by the congregation. (The two aren't necessarily always one and the same.) If the people are singing in unison, why not do something else? Consider what happens to "Amazing Grace" by borrowing Handel's "Thanks Be to Thee" pulsing harmony under a long and drawn out melody:

Example 5.1. "Amazing Grace," Tune: NEW BRITAIN, W. Walker, *Southern Harmony*, 1835.

On another occasion that hymn may be sung entirely unaccompanied, all four stanzas. Perhaps this could be established by having stanza one sung by a soloist a cappella. Have the organist leave the bench to visually communicate that the organ will not be jumping in. The hymn is truly to be without accompaniment. An incorrect assumption we make is that any given song HAS TO HAVE accompaniment. Sometimes no accompaniment will help the singing the most.

On yet another occasion, that same hymn ("Amazing Grace") may be accompanied with a Black-Gospel piano or blues style.

In all these cases one thing remains constant: the congregation sings the melody and text.

How do you decide when to do varied accompaniments, and when is it appropriate, so that you do not create a dog-and-pony show?

Sometimes varying the accompaniment can be purely for the sake of surprise, or for the sake of variety as described with "Amazing Grace" above. None of the accompaniments really have a direct tie to the words of that hymn (although I can imagine having some fun with the "wretch" part!). Also, so many different cultures and musical styles claim that hymn, that it is hard to uncover the "true" style. (There may not be one.)

Often, however, decisions about how to accompany a hymn beyond a four-part setting are related to what culture and time the hymn comes from, and whether a different accompaniment can help the melody and its text flow together better. History suggests various singing practices; global and/or ethnic origin suggests different practices. Your space and instruments suggest different practices. They all play a part.

I think the worst thing we could do is to treat every congregational song as a northern European chorale regardless of when and where the hymn comes from. For example:

Example 5.2. "Of the Father's Love Begotten," as chorale.
Tune: DIVINUM MYSTERIUM, plainsong, mode V, 13th century.

This chant would find its truer voice when accompanied as follows:

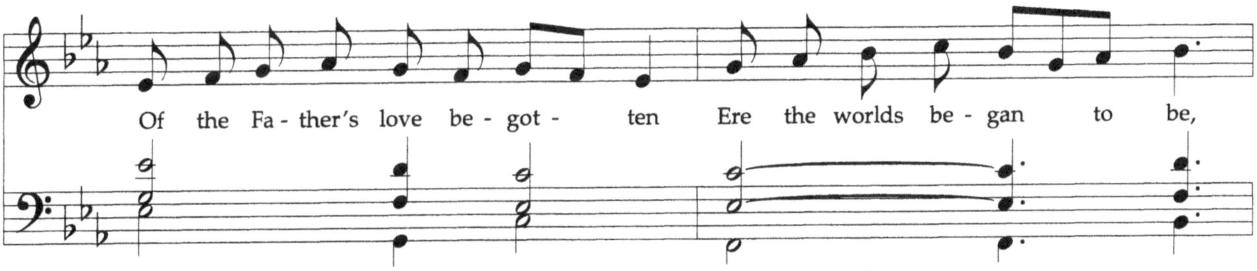

Example 5.3. "Of the Father's Love Begotten," as chant.

This manner brings out the melodic and nonmetric nature of these mysterious chant melodies. We are naturally drawn to the phrase instead of each chord.

DIFFERENT STROKES FROM DIFFERENT FOLKS

The organ and beyond...

The church in the 20th century has experienced a literal explosion of its song. Songs are coming from all over the globe, and the Church is experiencing new kinds of expressions that don't sound like northern Europe anymore. To force a South African freedom song onto the organ is a sure fire way to discourage good participation.

Someone recently asked me if I thought the organ was going to go the way of the typewriter. I said "No," but of course I'm biased—I am an organist, for crying out loud! But that's not why I said no. I believe congregations will continue to install good pipe organs because no other instrument can do what the pipe organ does for song: express the full range of the texts in song, and do it acoustically (without electronic enhancement). I hope and believe that the Church will again some day say it is OK to have an instrument that is indeed unique to the Church and is not found in every corner bar. We organists have to be patient and hang in there.

What I think is and will be increasingly different in times to come, though, is that the organ is going to have company in its role in assisting the congregation in their song. Percussion instruments such as piano and rhythm instruments (conga drums, guiro, shakers, etc., but not the trap set[1]) are on the increase as they too can lead larger gatherings.

Organists have to learn when to slide off the organ bench and onto another "bench" since the song is the point, not the instrument that carries it. Many of the songs we are assimilating into our repertoire are better encouraged with an instrument other than organ.

If we understand accompaniment as "up for grabs" and permission to consider other ways of accomplishing the accompaniment with many instruments, we will assist these newer songs (and some older songs) in becoming ever more vital! And most likely in the process, we will learn new ways to use the organ.

In devising an accompaniment to a tune and text, there are three things to consider: 1) rhythm, 2) harmonic treatment (accompaniment figures), and 3) the instrumentation itself.

CREATIVE IDEAS FOR ORGAN ACCOMPANIMENT

I still believe the organ to be one of the best instruments for leading larger groups in song. It produces sound the same way as the human voice—air vibrating in a tube, and it can lead larger groups with natural acoustic sound similar to congregations having an entire symphony at their disposal.

The most frequent method of accompaniment with organ is to indeed play four-part settings. It makes sense, as this tradition comes from the same place as the organ: Europe. But there is more for you to add to organ accompaniments:

◆ 1. Improvise your own harmonies. (See part two of this book!)

◆ 2. Play some stanzas without pedal.

◆ 3. Use pedal point—plant a foot on tonic or dominant, play harmonies from the hymnal with the hands. Keep your foot there until you can't stand it any more, then switch back to the pedal line in the book.

◆ 4. Try fewer chords. Especially with early American hymns, you only need to play the chords written on the downbeat and/or strong beat of each measure. Do not use a new chord for every beat.

[1]Trap sets are what throw the natural balance off! The minute a group adds a trap set with a full set of cymbals and snare drum, everything else needs a microphone in order to match the decibel level. Perhaps this would be OK if you hand out microphones to all worshipers who come! Otherwise, there is an unnatural balance.

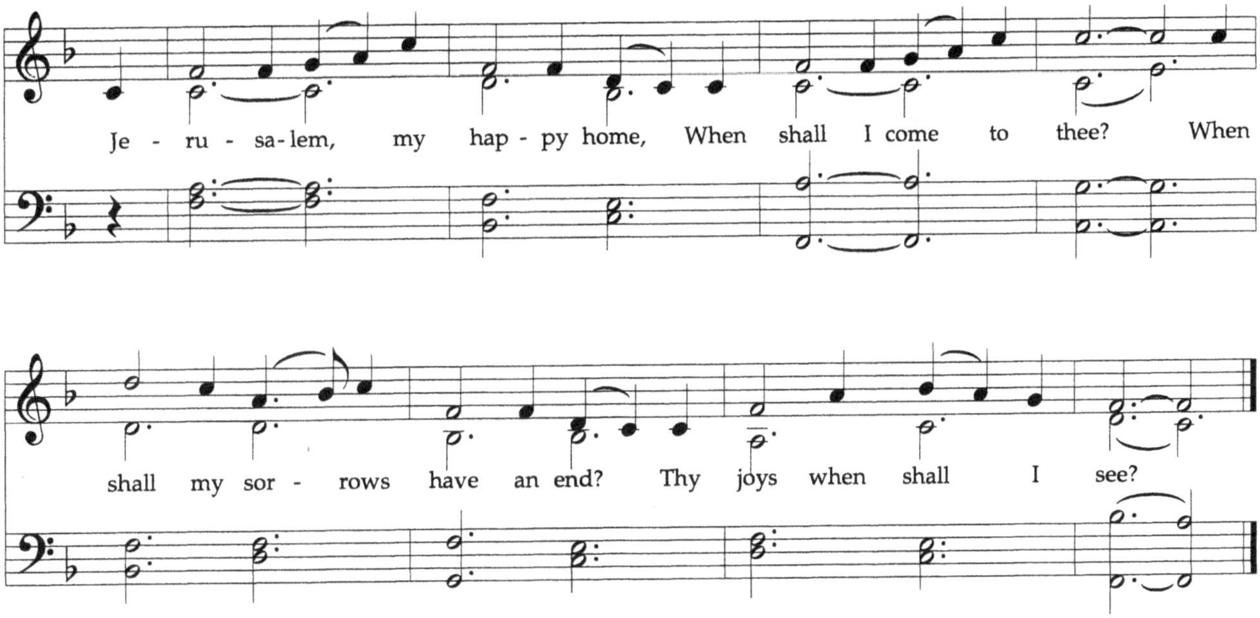

Example 5.4. "Jerusalem, My Happy Home," Text: F. B. P., 16th century. Tune: LAND OF REST, American folk tune.

◆ 5. Alternate unison and harmony.

◆ 6. Play a fourth below the melody. Leave everything else the same.

this:

can become this:

Example 5.5. "Sing Praise to God the Highest Good," Tune: LOBT GOTT DEN HERREN, IHR, Melchior Vulpius, c. 1560–1615.

◆ 7. Ostinato, such as the following:

Example 5.6. "Lord, Whose Love in Humble Service," Tune: BEACH SPRING, *The Sacred Harp*, Philadelphia, 1844.

◆ 8. Sustain chords under the melody. This is especially helpful for hymns of chant origin, like "Of the Father's Love Begotten." (See example 5.3)

◆ 9. Fill in melodic thirds in any voice (including soprano).

Example 5.7. "Now Thank We All Our God," Tune: NUN DANKET ALLE GOTT, Johann Crüger, 1598–1662.

An important consideration is that the organ produces continuous tone. You do not have to restrike the key to rekindle the tone. It plays as long as you hold the key down. This is good to remember when you translate "piano" music to the organ. A quick look at the organ arrangement of Malotte's "The Lord's Prayer" compared to the piano, demonstrates how a sustained chord replaces piano arpeggios. Both arrangements accomplish sustained harmony, but do so differently in relation to the nature of the instrument being played.

Hymns from the ages can suggest different things on the organ. Here are four different styles of hymnody that can be led with organ. As Alice Parker admonishes us, read the small print. From when and where did the hymn come to us, and how might it have sounded in its original setting?

Chant is demonstrated above. Sustained accompaniment with few harmonic changes helps bring out the melismatic beauty and mystery of these nonmetric tunes. (Actually, using a cappella unison would be best—especially if the acoustics are live.)

Renaissance hymns, such as "In Thee Is Gladness" should be light and airy. Consider the madrigal, "Now Is the Month of Maying." You certainly don't get a feel similar to a Bach chorale!

Example 5.8. "In Thee Is Gladness," Tune: IN DIR IST FREUDE, Giovanni Giacomo Gastoldi, c. 1556–1622.

The original pre-Bach chorales are renaissance music and are very dancelike. One usually can also find a "hemiola." Hemiola is dancing three steps where you would normally dance two. Look for hemiolas, and if found, bring them out if you can, or at least "think" them.

$\frac{6}{8}$ time:	1	2	3	4	5	6
Normal:	Step	—	—	Step	—	—
Hemiola:	**Step**	**—**	**Step**	**—**	**Step**	**—**
Normal:	Com-	—	fort	Com-	—	fort
Hemiola:	**now**	**my**	**peo-**	**—**	**ple.**	**—**

Hemiolas may be brought out in the accompaniment:

Example 5.9. "Comfort, Comfort Now My People," Text: Johann Olearius, 1611–84; tr. Catherine Winkworth, 1829–78. alt. Tune: FREU DICH SEHR, *Trente quatre pseaumes de David*, Geneva, 1551.

"A Mighty Fortress" in the original rhythm should be light, yet firm, most chords separated with great energy:

Example 5.10. "A Mighty Fortress Is Our God," Text and tune: EIN FESTE BURG, Martin Luther, 1483–1546.

With renaissance tunes and German chorales, I always imagine what the instrument of music in that time may have been. I think of recorders and krummhorns, homophonically played chord to chord—playfully. I keep that character in my head and in the articulation while playing.

Great Britain. I get an image of the English Cathedral with its 7 seconds of reverberation, the great depth in tempo and sound, great big fat reeds without mixtures perhaps, and the clear 4/4 majestic rhythm of a procession. Quite different from the dance music of the Renaissance just discussed. The British style is legato, flowing, yet firm with great breadth. Notice how the harmonization brings out 4/4, and uses new chords for almost every beat.

Example 5.11. "Praise, My Soul, the King of Heaven," Text: Henry F. Lyte, 1793–1847.
Tune: PRAISE, MY SOUL, John Goss, 1800–80.

"Holy, Holy, Holy" (NICAEA) falls into this camp—thick majestic 4/4 processional image.

French. There are a few. NOËL NOUVELET comes to mind—often with the text "Now the Green Blade Rises." This too should be light and full of space. Perhaps not playing a chord every beat:

Example 5.12. "Now the Green Blade Rises," Tune: NOËL NOUVELET, French carol.

There are many other examples of hymns that can find their best expression with the help of the organ. They make up the majority of the Church's current hymnody. They include both historic western hymns and a good portion of that which has been written in contemporary society following this style. Much of the new hymnody has come to us by Europe's ancestors living in all parts of the globe. I've used the above types as examples since they represent a good number of styles and demonstrate how hymns can be treated differently with the organ. There are certainly many more styles than I've listed, but the point has been made.

Time to move on to the organ's new partners.

THE PIANO

Next to the organ, the piano is the most frequently used instrument for leading song. It is important to remember that the piano is a percussion instrument. That is to say, it produces tone by striking something. (The hammer strikes the string and the sound decays.) This is quite different from the organ or the human voice. It is also one instrument; unlike the organ, the piano has only one sound. Variation is achieved through dynamics, phrasing and "voicing" (i.e., which octave you play), and the arrangements themselves. Being aware of this helps inform the musician about the use of the instrument.

There are many types of congregational song in our ecumenical repertoire that truly are better led with piano than organ. This could include, but is not limited to:

19th century Gospel music, like "Precious Lord," "Blessed Assurance," etc., which, given the relatively few harmonic changes, are greatly helped by the percussive nature of the piano.

African American spirituals. These are also effective a cappella, or with other instrumentation, but I tend to prefer the piano for them.

Folk music from the 60s and 70s such as "Seek Ye First the Kingdom of God."

Modern Black-Gospel, such as "Soon and Very Soon."

Hispanic Music. Piano alone works very well, but Hispanic music, at its best, is led by an ensemble, perhaps including piano as only one of many instruments.

Contemporary pop-style such as the music of Sandi Patti or Handt Hansen.

Each of these styles call for very different treatment on the keyboard, or piano—none of them the four-part settings as you will find in the hymnal. In many such hymns, the best treatment would be for keyboard or piano to be one of several accompanying instruments, but my hunch is that often it's you and the piano alone that need to make these songs work.

"Help!" you say? "I've only learned to play the four-part settings. What do I do?"

GETTING STARTED ON THE PIANO

So often we hear of pianists who get drafted to play the organ. Seldom do we hear of the other way around—the organist being told to play the piano as well! I think this is going to become more common as new songs make their way into our repertoire.

Our training as organists teaches us primarily (but not entirely) to recreate printed music, and make music alone as a solo performer. It's time to go beyond, in this case, with the piano. When we translate four-part music to the piano we are already "transcribing." Four-part writing is mostly "vocal," intended for four parts: soprano, alto, tenor, and bass. The organ represents these well, as the organ is also vocal. However, piano, being a percussion instrument, is slightly different. We certainly can play merely the four-parts as written, and, if clearly played with good tactus and breathing, that can be quite sufficient. However, much more can be done. We must learn to improvise from that which is on the page to make full and efficient use of the piano—a percussion instrument with an extensive range of pitches! And often the piano makes up for instruments that may not be available such as bass, additional percussion, and possibly melody instruments.

Certainly this book will not alone provide you with the skills to improvise, but you can get a good start.

When I was in the band, and we were learning new songs, we didn't buy the sheet music. We bought the recording and learned the songs by ear. This you can do too. Get the sounds in your ears. If you want to learn Black-Gospel, get some recordings of leading artists, then listen and imitate. Crudely to be sure, but imitate!

Or, look at some published things and apply similar treatments in another key, then another hymn.

"Imitate?" you say, "I can't even play middle C without seeing it on the page." Where do we begin?

Here are some starting ideas. We'll come back to the imitating issue.

Who says all notes of a chord have to be played at the same time? Remember that the piano is a percussion instrument, and that its sound is maintained by restriking the string. A harmony can be sustained by making use of a famous piano tool: the arpeggio.

Example 5.13. C major chord becomes arpeggio.

You can read from the hymnal, playing the chords of the printed accompaniment, but arpeggiating them.

Example 5.14."Amazing Grace," Tune: NEW BRITAIN, William Walker, *Southern Harmony,* 1835.

This is a start. Now write a folk melody with guitar chords on staff paper. As you play the melody arpeggiate the guitar chords beneath it.

You're on your way because much of what comes next in this book builds on this.

From there you can develop a set of "licks,"—notes that go beyond mere arpeggios. You develop a repertoire of them, one at a time, and find the right place to plug them in.

Let's apply what I mean through exploring several types of music for which I would accompany with the piano.

Folk music

In folk music, especially from the 60s and early 70s, the instrument of choice was the guitar, and the preferred setting, of course, the campfire. Guitar may indeed work, but for larger groups one might need a guitar **CHOIR** to make it work. You can't duplicate the campfire. Anyway, here you are now 30 or more years later at the piano with the same music. Think guitar. A good guitar player picks the chords like Alberti bass or arpeggios (or imagine how a harpist would do it), not the amateur guitar "da-di-da-di-da-da." Nicely plucked chords are established.

"Seek Ye First," with a very basic 4-part accompaniment may look like this in the hymnal:

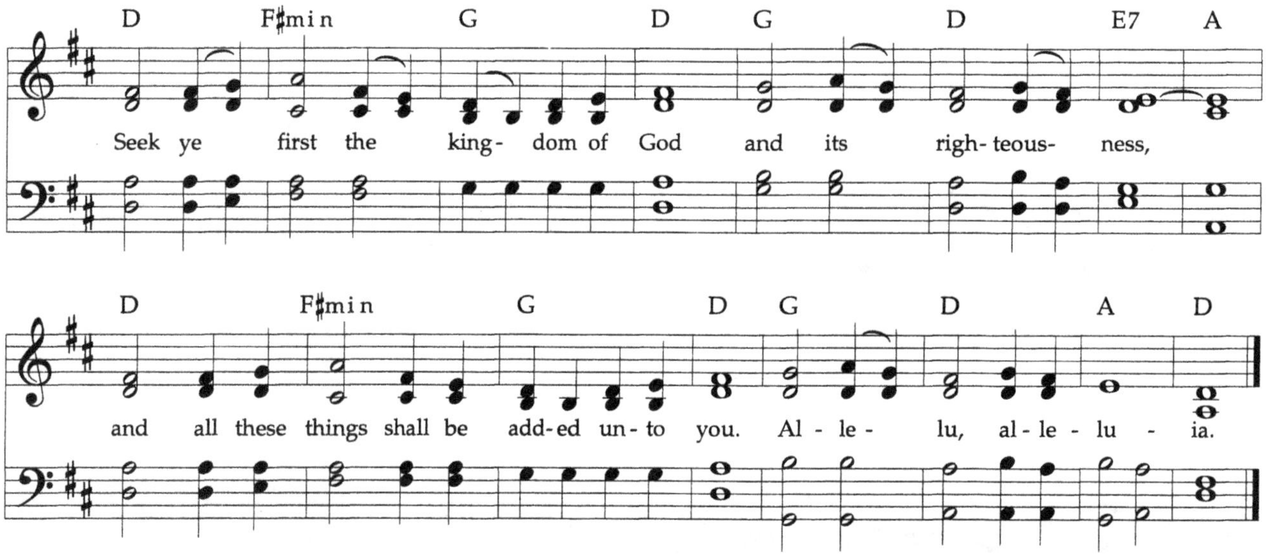

Example 5.15. "Seek Ye First," 4-part setting. Text: Matt. 6:33, adapt. Karen Lafferty, b. 1948.
Tune: LAFFERTY, Karen Lafferty, © 1972 Maranatha! Music, administered by The Copyright Co., Nashville, TN.

For this song, written in the era of the 60s and 70s, I imagine a guitar by a campfire, "picking" the strings instead of strumming chords. I devise an accompaniment by thinking guitar while at the piano by looking at the guitar chords written above (as is most often the case with this style of music), and merely arpeggiating those chords below the melody, it becomes:

Example 5.16. "Seek Ye First," piano imitating guitar.

If the guitar chords are not provided, figure some out—one chord per measure, perhaps two.

Hymn tunes by the well-known contemporary composer Marty Haugen can use the same treatment:

"Gather Us In" by Marty Haugen printed in basic form might look like this:

Example 5.17. "Gather Us In," Text and tune: Marty Haugen, b. 1950. © 1982, GIA Publications, Inc.

By thinking guitar and arpeggiating with the left hand, the accompaniment can become:

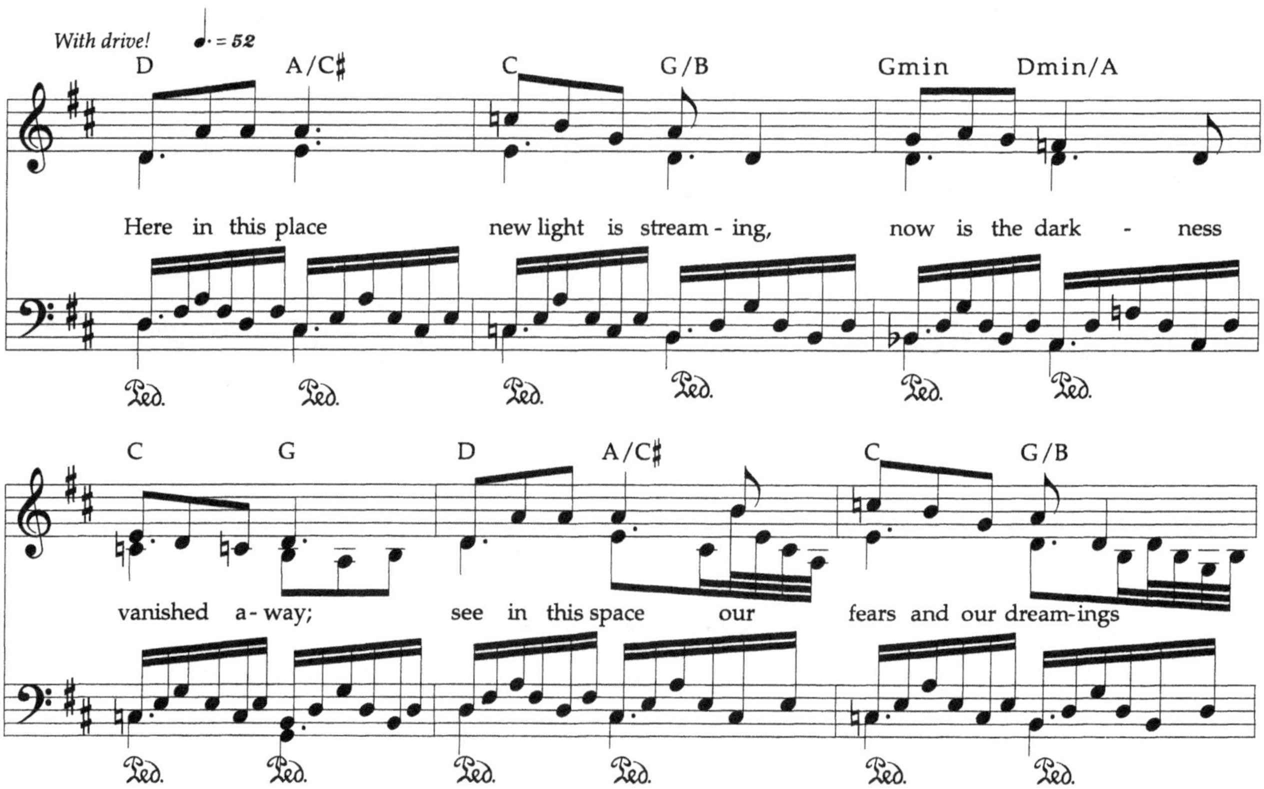

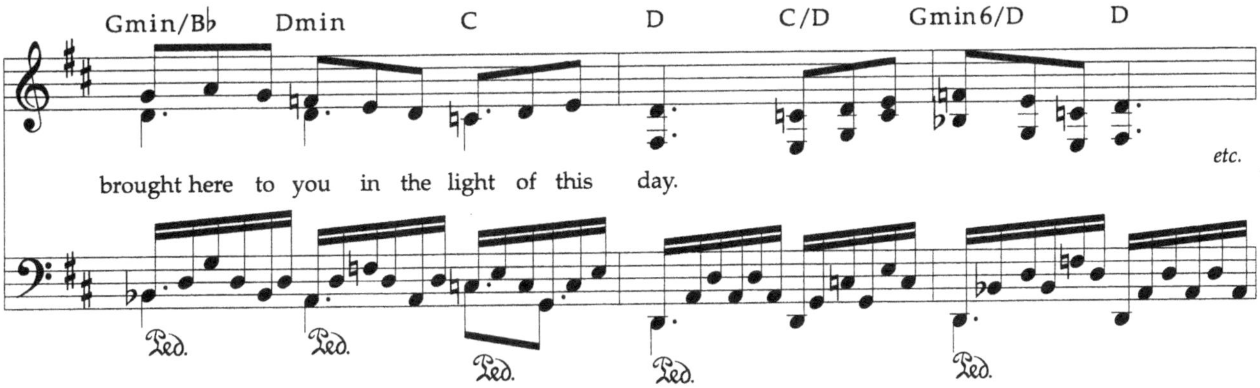

Example 5.18. "Gather Us In," imitating guitar.

Let's apply the same technique to a "traditional hymn" for illustrative purposes. In one hymnal, this hymn looks like this:

Example 5.19. "Your Kingdom Come, O Father," Text: Kauko-Veikko Tamminen, 1882–1946; tr. Ernest E. Ryden, b. 1886, © 1970 Lutheran World Federation. Tune: Finnish folk tune.

Reading the small print, I noticed that it is a Finnish FOLK tune. I thought guitar again—or at least something quite different than four-part writing. By arpeggiating the harmonies, one gets quite a different feel, and the 5/4 measures are not so jarring:

Example 5.20. "Your Kingdom Come, O Father," Arrangement: David M. Cherwien, © 1992, Summa Productions, Minneapolis, MN 55414-1510.

Hispanic Songs

Thinking guitar leads us nicely into considering music from Hispanic cultures. One Sunday we had a group from a Hispanic ministries congregation in Minneapolis come and assist with our worship. There were no amplifiers, and surprisingly to me (a white, Scandinavian-Polish Lutheran), not a large number of drums. Most of the dozen or so instruments used were guitars of all sizes—all playing against each other in interesting rhythms. The feel was very relaxed yet celebratory. There was a conga or two and a guiro, but most of the percussive sound came from the guitars (also a percussion instrument). There was great emphasis on the UPBEAT, not the downbeat as most European musicians tend to feel. The hymn I especially remember was "Alabaré." What might this hymn accompaniment look like when the piano needs to be all of these instruments wrapped up into one?

"Alabaré" in a basic setting:

Example 5.21. "Alabaré," Text and tune © 1979, Manuel José Alonso and José Pagán y Ediciones Musical PAX. All rights reserved. Sole U.S. Agent; OCP Publications, 5536 NE Hassalo, Portland, OR 97213. Used with permission.

By "breaking up" the half-note chords, we can add some interest already. By doing so with off-beat rhythm we can add more. Here is what it can become by emphasizing the off-beat:

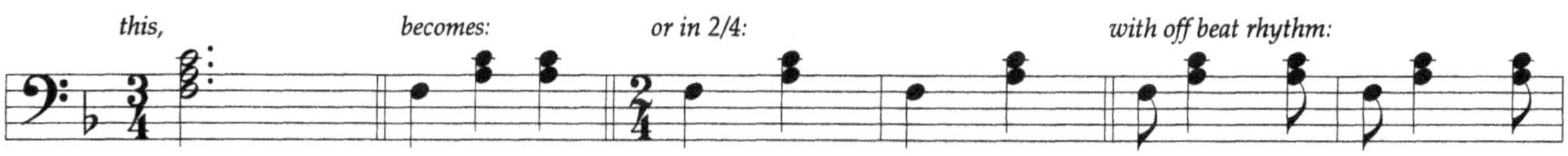

Example 5.22. Accompaniment figure.

Example 5.23. Applied to "Alabaré."Text and tune © 1979, Manuel José Alonso and José Pagán y Ediciones Musical PAX. All rights reserved. Sole U.S. Agent; OCP Publications, 5536 NE Hassalo, Portland, OR 97213. Used with permission.

Of course there is the well-known calypso figure:

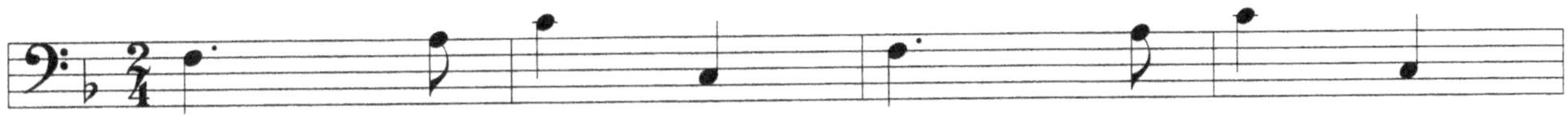

Example 5.24. Calypso figure.

Applied to "Alabaré" with all of the above:

Example 5.25. "Alabaré," with all of the above. Text and tune © 1979, Manuel José Alonso and José Pagán y Ediciones Musical PAX. All rights reserved. Sole U.S. Agent; OCP Publications, 5536 NE Hassalo, Portland, OR 97213. Used with permission.

Add an imaginary small Spanish guitar "lick."

Example 5.26. "Alabaré," with all of the above. Text and tune © 1979, Manuel José Alonso and José Pagán y Ediciones Musical PAX. All rights reserved. Sole U.S. Agent; OCP Publications, 5536 NE Hassalo, Portland, OR 97213. Used with permission.

At best you should have an ensemble of guitars and rhythm instruments when doing Hispanic music. When this is not possible, you need to imagine what such a group might sound like, and imitate it as closely as possible on the piano.

Continuing the thought of the piano imitation, think of this Jamaican folk tune, "Let Us Talents and Tongues Employ":

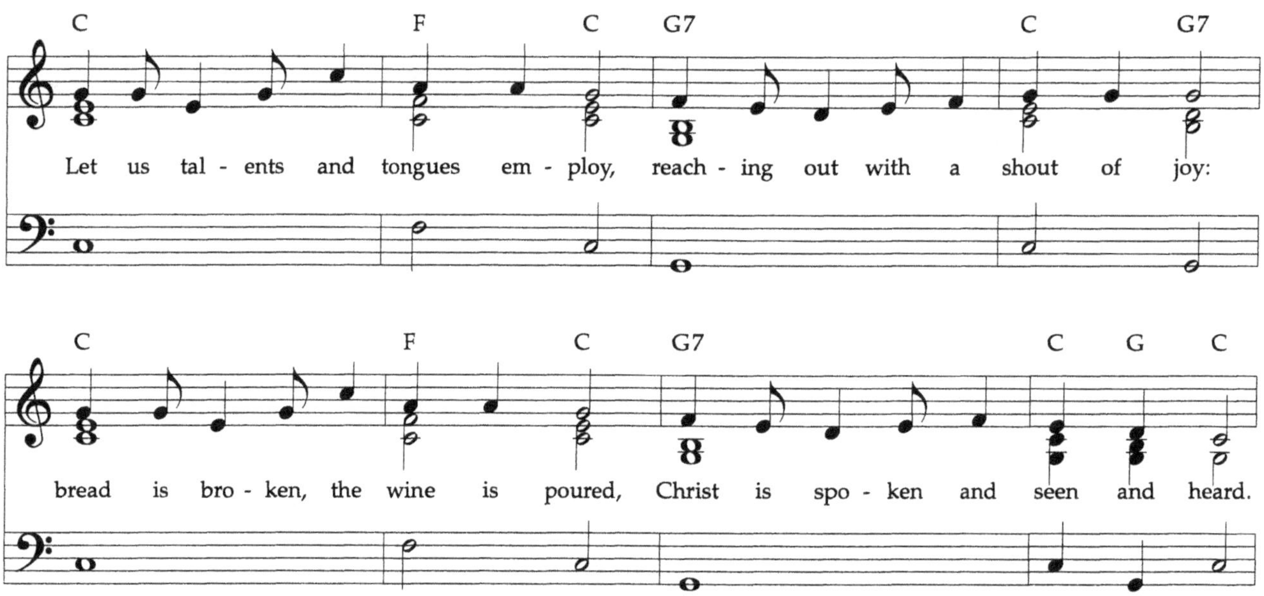

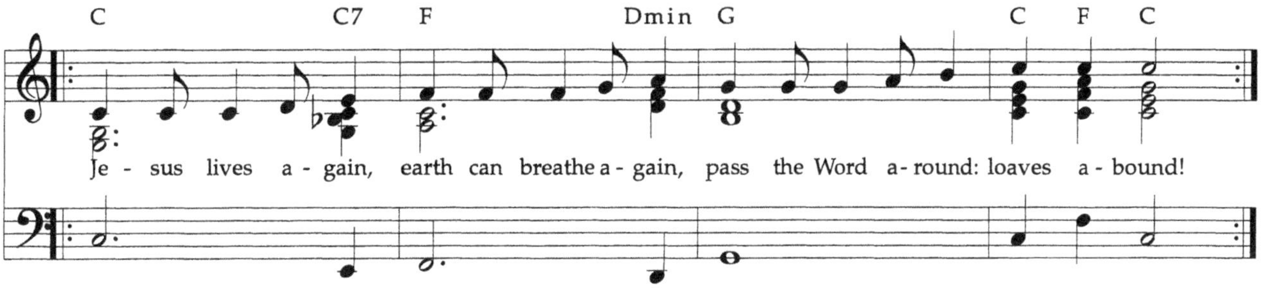

Example 5.27. "Let Us Talents and Tongues Employ," Text: Fred Kaan, b. 1929. Tune: LINSTEAD, Jamaican folk tune, adapt. Doreen Potter, 1925–80. Text and tune ©1975 Hope Publishing Co., Carol Stream, IL 60188.

Imagining percussion (again, on the offbeat):

Example 5.28. "Let Us Talents and Tongues Employ," with wild accompaniment.

If the singing is going well, it could be that you no longer need to pamper the congregation with the notes of the melody all the time. Then you are free to emphasize percussive "licks," and harmonies, perhaps only now and then hinting at the melody:

Example 5.29. "Let Us Talents and Tongues Employ," without always playing the melody.

Black-Gospel

Black-Gospel piano playing has long infatuated me. It is clearly a style of its own. Those who grow up in this style seem to feel it naturally. The rest of us have a lot to learn! It is indeed learnable, as I have found upon studying it, listening to it, working with it, and playing together with experts. There is indeed a language to it made up of "licks" to apply appropriately. One basic difference to European hymnody is the emphasis on the offbeats as opposed to the downbeats.

Let's study a well-known example of Black-Gospel, and identify some "licks":

Example 5.30. "Amazing Grace," arr. John Coates, Jr., © 1971 Shawnee Press, Inc., (ASCAP)

Notice the "triplets" in a 3/4 meter. This is very common, as in jazz. Notice the grace notes "sliding up" to a major third by an immediate lower neighbor a half-step lower. Notice the heavy use of the seventh, the "licks" in measures 3 to 4 in the right hand, and the chromatic passing tones of measure 4.

From looking at various examples, listening to Black-Gospel, and experimenting, I have developed a repertoire of "licks" which I insert from time to time. Let me share a few of these with you to illustrate what to look for. Try them yourself. Play each of them in a number of keys. Look for places to insert them with hymns you may play in this style.

◆ 1. Instead of straight quarter pulses, feel a set of triplets in each beat.

Example 5.31. Transforming the straight beat into triplets.

Example 5.32. "Amazing Grace," first in straight pulses, then with triplets for each beat.

Jazz musicians do this as a rule. When writing out this style of music I would have to change 3/4 meter to 12/8 so that each pulse included three eighth notes (the same as triplets). In "Amazing Grace" of Example 5.30, the composer actually writes them as triplets and keeps the 3/4 meter. In Example 5.38 below, "Go Down, Moses," I actually changed the meter to 12/8. Having to do things like turn 4/4 into 12/8 points out how difficult it is to notate a style that is intrinsically improvisational.

◆ 2. To prolong any one chord, you can "walk" up to the seventh and then back down. This can be done with the left hand or the right hand, or combined. This particular "lick" can be accomplished a large number of ways. Here are some examples:

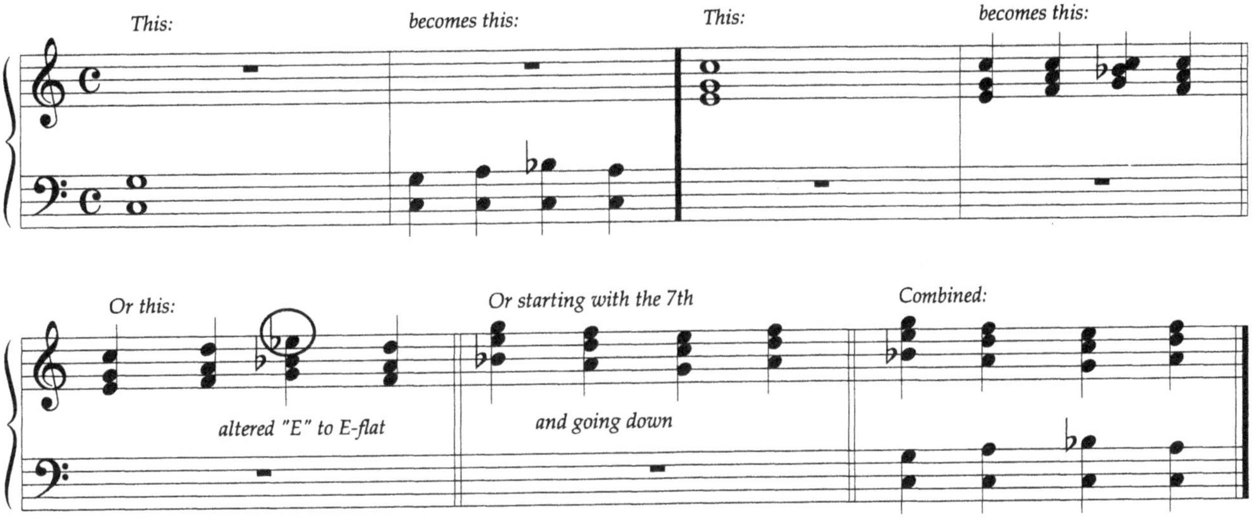

Example 5.33. "Walking" up to the seventh.

◆ 3. "Walking" six-four chords. This "lick" can be used in prolonging the same chord, or in approaching a chord.

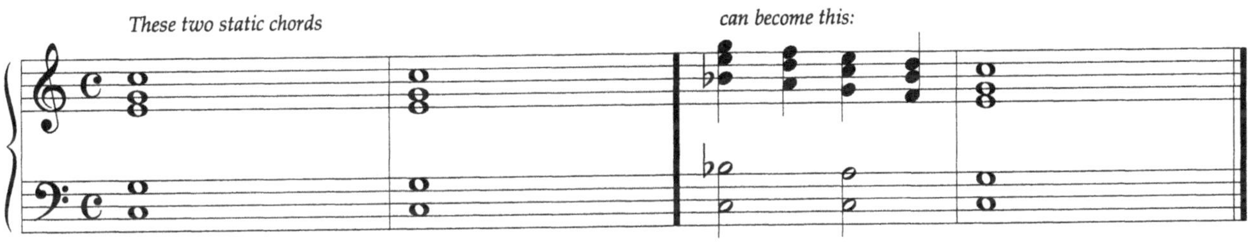

Example 5.34. "Walking" six-four chords approaching a chord.

◆ 4. Upper neighbor chords, as if to do a mini I-IV-I progression instead of repeated static chords.

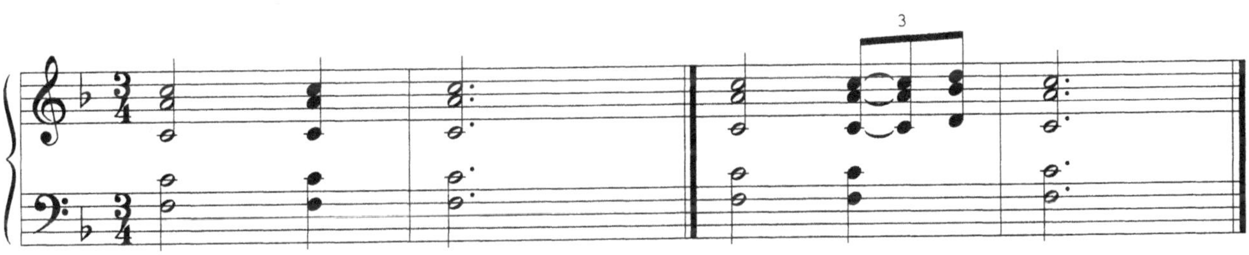

Example 5.35. Upper neighbor I-IV-I progression.

◆ 5. Moving up stepwise, adding a flatted third, either within one beat, or stretched throughout an entire measure. This is especially useful when the harmony is moving up a fourth. This "lick" ends on the "leading tone" to the goal.

Example 5.36. Moving up stepwise adding a flatted third.

◆ 6. Approaching any chord with a melodic lick—playing notes 5-6-1-1 of the scale.

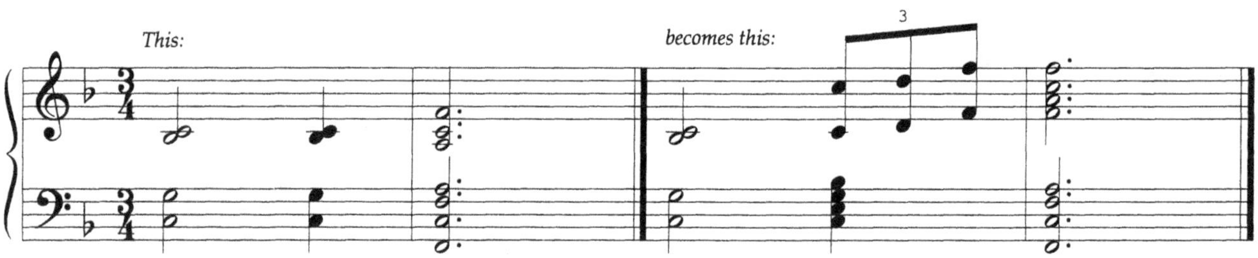

Example 5.37. Approaching a chord with a melodic "lick" 5-6-1-1.

Let's put some of these into the spiritual accompaniment of, "Go Down, Moses." See if you can identify some of the above licks in this example.

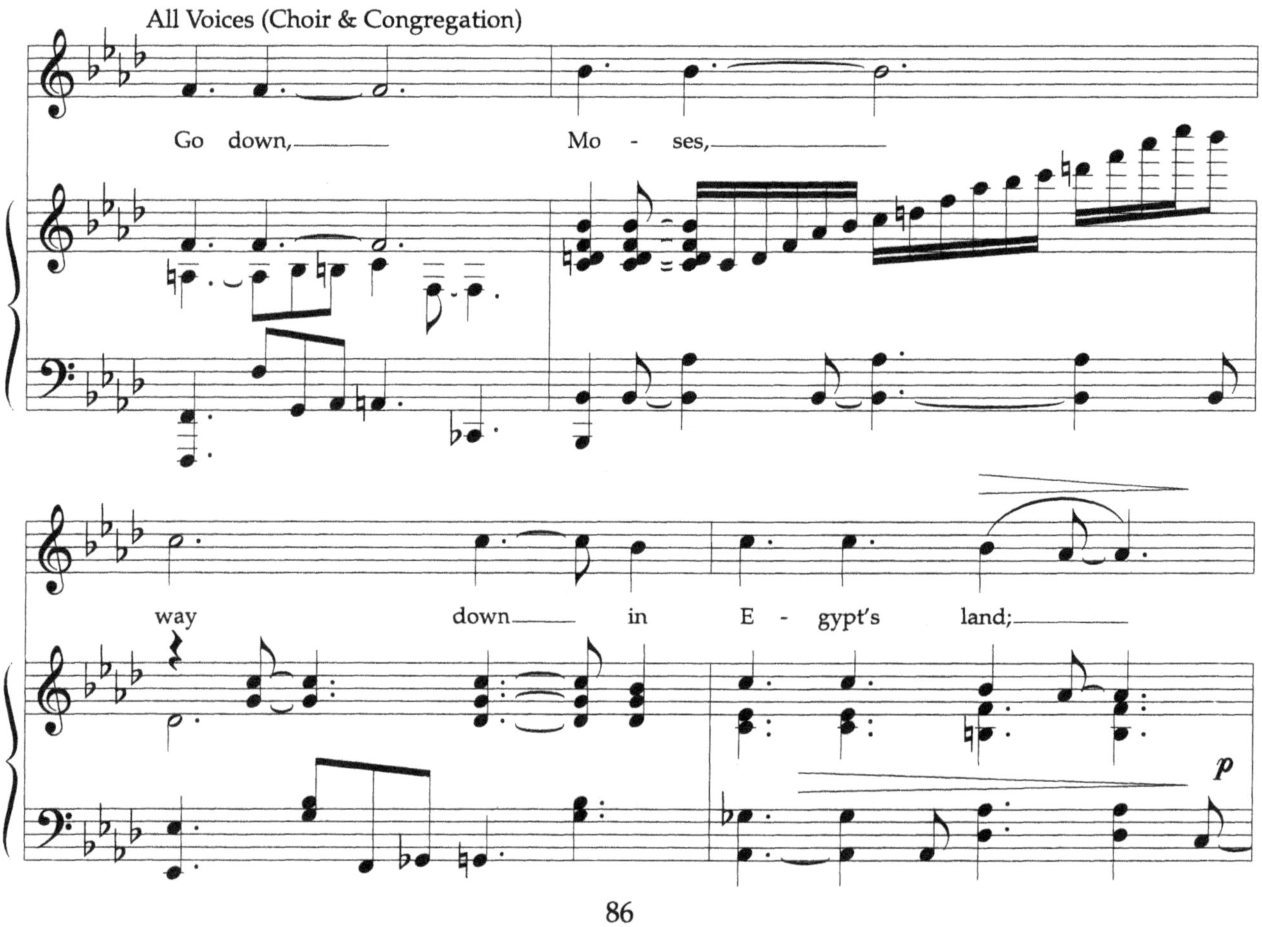

Example 5.38. "Go Down, Moses," African American spiritual, Arrangement: David M. Cherwien, © 1992 The Evangel Press, a division of Summa Productions, Minneapolis, MN 55414-1510.

Consider "What a Fellowship," first as I imagine traditional 19th century white pioneers moving across the frontier sang and played it on the piano:

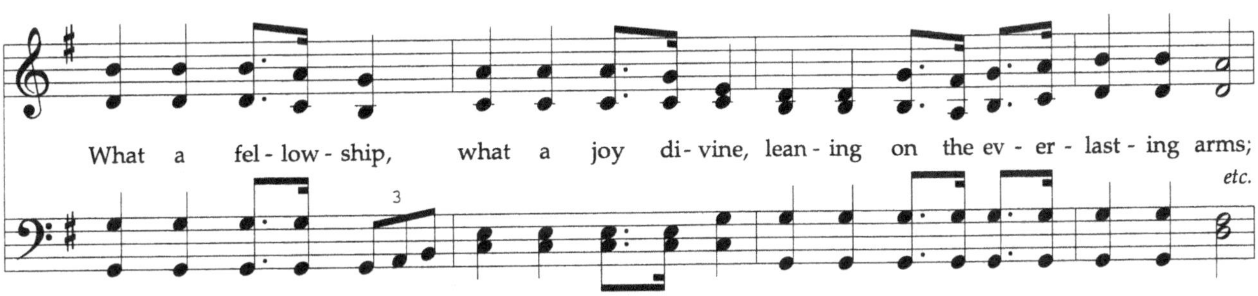

Example 5.39. "What a Fellowship, What a Joy Divine," Text: Elisha Hoffman, 1839–1929. Tune: SHOWALTER. Anthony J. Showalter, 1858–1924.

When played in a Black-Gospel sound, upbeats are emphasized, some "licks" are inserted, and it becomes:

Example 5.40. "What a Fellowship," á la Black-Gospel.

19th Century Gospel

These include hymns like "Blessed Assurance," "Precious Lord," "Softly and Tenderly," "Rock of Ages," etc. These hymns need the percussion of the piano, as there are usually only three main chords and lots of harmonic repetition which works on the piano. In my imagining of the original style, we do go back to emphasizing the downbeat, but with a gentle lilt. The tactus is really a dotted half note, with the ♩. = 58 in this example:

Example 5.41. "Blessed Assurance," Text: Fanny J. Crosby, 1820–1915.
Tune: ASSURANCE, Phoebe P. Knapp, 1830–1908.

It can be dressed up a bit with left hand octaves to emphasize the down beat, and with some "licks" borrowed from Black-Gospel style. This brings out beats 2 and 3 (the off beats!), and gives a different tactus—not the dotted quarter, but feeling a stronger eighth note. I love the "lilt" that this provides.

Example 5.42. "Blessed Assurance," dressed up.

Given that these are harmonically simple (usually three chords: tonic I, sub-dominant IV, and dominant V) you can just keep a chord in your mind, and use all 88 keys—especially once the congregation gets going on the melody and doesn't really need you to be playing the melody itself. Don't worry, they'll carry it. They may not even notice that you aren't playing the melody. If the absence of the melody on the keyboard makes you nervous, get a saxophone player to play it.

So, here's yet one more level of "Blessed Assurance," implying the melody without hitting everyone with it between the eyes:

fore - taste of glo-ry di - vine! Heir of sal - va - tion, pur-chase of
God, born of his Spir - it, washed in his blood. This is my
sto - ry, this is my song, prais - ing my

Example 5.43. "Blessed Assurance," "dressed to the hilt!" Arrangement: David M. Cherwien.

Spirituals

These are one of the greatest gifts to the Church in the last 100+ years. These songs can flourish in their unadorned original very-free form, light and without any accompaniment. Yet, the integrity of these songs sung by slaves full of hope and trust for freedom from oppression, is so great that they seem to withstand just about any treatment. A fugue on "Steal Away" may seem out of place, but I can imagine it working.

I especially became interested in piano treatment of spirituals when I heard a CD of Barbara Hendricks and a Russian pianist.[2] The story told on the CD cover states that while they were on a concert tour they were simply killing time one day. She started singing spirituals; he began improvising with her. Someone overheard them, and the result is this CD. The piano playing is exquisite—a true crossing of jazz, gospel and Beethoven. Not an unnecessary or uncontrolled note, and interesting arrangements, to be sure.

I began experimenting and discovered how wonderfully spirituals work for congregational settings with this style of accompaniment. Hence, "Nobody Knows the Trouble I've Seen" can become a New Orleans Jazz style:

[2]*Barbara Hendricks Sings Spirituals.* Barbara Hendricks, soprano, and Demitri Alexeev, piano. EMI Records, Hayes Middlesex, England. ©1983. Catalogue number CDC 747 0262.

Example 5.44. "Nobody Knows the Trouble I've Seen," Arrangement: David M. Cherwien.
© 1994, The Evangel Press, an affiliate of AMSI, Minneapolis, MN 55414-1510.

By now you are noticing the "licks," learned from other styles and applied here.

Jazz

We don't have a lot of true jazz tunes that are sung in church (at least not at this time). I would not be surprised if they were to come soon. I do not discuss jazz at length here as there are many jazz pedagogy books. In fact, I would bet that you would have an easier time finding one of these than you would an edition of Bach's Two-Part Inventions.

You might find these jazz books very helpful, as they contain numerous "scales" and exercises that teach precisely what I have been describing here: "licks." You can develop some from these books, then find places to apply them as an exercise.

Piano is indeed a needed instrument with many "contemporary" songs being added to our repertoire, and the skills in using piano effectively now need to be added to our ever-growing list of required abilities as the church's leaders of song.

Perhaps the greatest difficulty in using piano is that with very large groups (over 200), it is still difficult for all to hear the piano. We need churches to get as large a piano as possible, leave the top open, and place the piano so that the sound goes directly into the space, not toward a wall. I would not amplify the piano, as that moves it into the realm of the unreal—out of proportion to the naturally produced (unamplified) human voice. If a microphone is perceived to be needed, I would see to it that everyone who attends worship that day also gets a microphone or I would not select songs that depend on piano.

PERCUSSION

I thought it was an expensive impulse on my part to buy a set of conga drums. A friend told me of a supplier with very low prices, so I picked up the phone and ordered a set without any idea how I would be using them. When they came, I called a young high school percussionist and told him to take them home and play with them. Six months later I saw them again. By now this young person had assembled a group of buddies who would go under a bridge together and improvise with their drums. He was an expert! He now owns his own set and plays them professionally.

My total surprise was how many of our new songs were helped by these drums! We are seeing a tremendous increase in the Church of songs from the African, Hispanic and South American cultures for which the accompaniment should be primarily percussion.

Think about it: a large drum can keep a huge gathering in touch with the tactus. Add more drums to it in counterpoint, and we have an extremely interesting accompaniment! What's missing is the actual singing itself. For this music initially, it is indeed extremely helpful to have a group of people leading it vocally (four or more) without microphones. "We Are Marching in the Light of God" could have such an accompaniment.

The foundation beat:

Example 5.45. Foundation.

Add the counterpoint:

Example 5.46. Counterpoint added with shakers, conga drums and clavés.

Add voices. Watch it happen.

Example 5.47. "We Are Marching in the Light of God," SIYAHAMBA. Text and Music: South African.

You can get away with just a set of conga drums; at best, add to that a large drum for the tactus, adding clavé sticks, guiro, and other percussion instruments in counterpoint. Mark Bangert, of the Lutheran School of Theology, Chicago, who traveled to Africa describes this "counterpoint" as drummers beginning with a pulse, then others filling in spaces. The more drummers there are, the fewer spaces there are to fill in and the harder it gets, but certainly it's more interesting!

Experiment. Pull a group of people together to teach.

NO ACCOMPANIMENT
Gregorian Chants, Music of Taizé, Spirituals, Shape Note; Southern Harmony

Here is the most affordable method of accompaniment: NO ACCOMPANIMENT!

That does not make it the easiest, however! Sometimes it takes a while to get the congregation "off the bottle," that is to say, weaned from accompaniment. Remember "Happy Birthday"? No one depends on accompaniment for that song. It is just sung.

Congregations are much more capable of singing without accompaniment than we and they think. Often when I drop out for a stanza and let it float without accompaniment, people come up to me after the service and comment on how wonderful that was (although I'm not always sure how to take that).

There are many types of music that work best without any accompaniment. Some examples would be:

> **Gregorian Chant:** "O Come, O Come Emmanuel," "Of the Father's Love Begotten," "Creator of the Stars of Night," "Come Holy Ghost, Our Souls Inspire" are examples. Sing stanza one with a soloist or choir, to establish the sound. Have the organist stand away from the keyboard if it is visible. That announces visually that there will be no accompaniment. Perhaps some bells on a pentatonic scale could be added, ringing randomly, (i.e., in the E♭ major of "Of the Father's Love Begotten": E♭, F, G, B♭ and C in any octave. This combination sounds best when you use more of the higher bells, and fewer bells in lower octaves).
>
> It may be possible to add to your list of unaccompanied chant portions of the liturgy, such as the *Great Thanksgiving* or the *Kyrie.* Try them unaccompanied sometime when the singing is going well.
>
> **Music of Taizé:** These songs are used more and more frequently and are found in most of the major hymnals published in the 1980s and 1990s. They include favorites such as "Jesus, Remember Me," "Eat This Bread, Drink This Cup," "Veni Sancte Spiritus," etc. They come to us from a small monastic order in southern France near Cluny. People flock to this place from all over the world, to hear this music that was developed by Jacques Berthier with an intentional simplicity and integrity. Short biblical texts are sung over and over and over as montras. At their best, these songs remain unaccompanied, with added instruments only as obligato lines above the singing (provided in editions of Taizé music). Taizé works especially well during the distribution of bread and wine in the Eucharist, as people can continue to sing the songs even as they approach the altar.

Spirituals: (i.e., "Steal Away") As earlier stated, these were originally sung without accompaniment, so can it be today. Let the harmonies naturally erupt from the people.

Shape Note; Southern Harmony: There are groups of people all over the United States who gather for afternoons and sing these songs hour upon hour. And every year they gather in national conventions to sing these songs for days! When first introduced to this style, I was amazed at the depth and power of the singing. People sit in a square. They take turns leading. The leader stands in the middle and circulates eye contact around the square. There is always a strong two-beat pulse: up and down. Amazing energy! These include tunes such as HOLY MANNA, JEFFERSON, WONDROUS LOVE, and LAND OF REST. They work well in canon, and in their original settings—usually with the melody in the tenor.

My hunch is that often the greatest obstacle to unaccompanied singing is not the people, but the acoustics. In dry rooms, one hears only one's self and we're back to the DFA syndrome. People do not like to hear themselves sing solo. (Well, OK, maybe there are some exceptions to that proclamation.) The problem is that we then use the accompanying instruments to cover up that fact and in the process can cover up the singing as well.

Get rid of the carpet, the padded pews, the acoustical tile ceilings. Be at every meeting where acoustics are discussed. Engineers will sometimes refer to "great acoustics" and mean "as dry as possible." You need to be there to filibuster for live acoustics. EVERYTHING THE CONGREGATION PARTICIPATES IN WILL BE HELPED—speaking and singing. Preaching and spoken word from the chancel can be dealt with nowadays with sophisticated sound systems, and in this case the use of microphones is OK, as the preaching and spoken word from the chancel are usually "solo." The congregation does not need to match them in volume.

By now we have explored many, many facets to helping your congregation sing. In some cases, we can only scratch the surface; i.e., playing in different styles, etc. Yet, if anything, my hope is that you now realize that the congregation's song not only deserves, but demands careful and thoughtful preparation by us. I hope you at least feel a twinge of guilt if you simply show up on Sunday morning and ask, "What are the hymns today?" Accept not thy check.

Chapter 6

CODA:

Some Additional Thoughts

VARIETY STARTS WITH THE SELECTION PROCESS

Imagine a service with three hymns, and they are: "My Hope Is Built on Nothing Less" (to the tune MELITA), "O Day Full of Grace" (to the tune DEN SIGNEDE DAG), and "Jesus Christ Is Risen Today," (to the tune EASTER HYMN). Naturally these three would be unlikely in the same service, as they have such different themes in their texts. But all three are in C major, all three are very strong, using primarily quarter notes, and all three begin with the triad!

It is important to think variety when *selecting* hymns for an entire service. For this reason, it is best when one person coordinates selection of all the hymns for a given service. If all three are the same structure, same fullness, same key, you have monotony. The large picture needs to be remembered.

There are many issues to remember when picking hymns for a service: the scriptural emphasis, the Church Year, the people, the worship space and its acoustics, the instruments, choir and congregational repertoire, and others.

Beside these issues the following should be kept in mind to avoid all of the hymns being the same:

- styles (historic era, ethnic origin)
- key and/or basic range of the melody
- tactus, meter, and/or rhythmic character
- texture (light or thick quarter note)
- melodic shape (are all the starting and ending ranges too low or too high?)
- mood of the text and tune
- tempo

There may be times when the desired effect is NOT to have the full variety. A Good Friday Service of Darkness may never lead into a bouncy joyous hymn. However, even on Easter, I try to find a hymn or two for the service that isn't all bombast! The break is refreshing, and it strengthens the bombast when we get back to it.

FLOW OF THE SERVICE

It is also important to keep in mind what precedes a hymn and what comes after it. The selection and your vision of how it will fit (including its introduction and how it is to be sung) need to flow out of what precedes it and point to that which follows, so that there is a continuous flow in the entire service, a continuous journey that begins with the prelude and ends with the last notes of the postlude. Within that larger journey are smaller journeys (such as within a hymn), but they are all integral and do not interrupt the larger journey. As an extreme example, it does not make sense to sing the hymn, "On Our Way Rejoicing, Gladly Let Us Go," as a processional hymn.

It is a tricky puzzle to fit all things together in a service so that they support each other, but it is worth the time and effort and should be a regular part of the musician's responsibilities. It is not helpful to just insert "favorites" in regular hymn slots in order to appease people. Hymns are selected because they are the precise piece for that spot of the puzzle. They fit and blend into the whole of the picture.

"FAMILIAR HYMNS, PLEASE"

A One, One-plus, One method

Most of the services I plan for have at least three hymns. They are usually 1) at the beginning, 2) right after the sermon, and 3) at the end in services without Holy Communion, or in services with Holy Communion, during distribution of the sacrament.

I try to follow the "One, One-plus, One" method when selecting hymns. One hymn in the service should be extremely well-known. One or more hymns should be fairly well-known, and finally, one hymn within the service can be a brand-new hymn. This way the well-known hymns soften the encounter with unknown hymns, and the regular encounter with unfamiliar hymns accustoms people to challenge. Avoiding "trying hymns on for size" and only singing the familiar are sure trips down lethargy lane. Without growth, there cannot be much life.

NEW HYMNS

Much can be done to help the first run of new hymns. I will certainly use the hymn's tune in the prelude, moving through the tune more than once in a variety of keys. I may use a slightly longer introduction (perhaps again going through the hymn a few times) with the melody very clearly given, and with tricky rhythmic spots clearly articulated. Having an instrumentalist play the tune in both the prelude and the introduction helps even more. When the singing begins, I will have the choir sing stanza one, the entire congregation stanza two, then the choir stanza three (to hear how stanza two was to have gone), and by stanza four the people know it. In this process we never have to hold up a banner in the chancel saying WARNING: NEW HYMN APPROACHING—YOU MAY WISH TO DUCK. Some may not have even noticed that it was a new hymn.

It is very important to remember the prophetic nature of the church musician. It is our duty to expose the people to new hymn possibilities in ways that are loving. But we can't expect them to jump up and down over the idea! Ignorant judgment can abound. Be patient. Give a new hymn two or three uses before deciding that it doesn't fit. Encourage music readers in the parish to do their part and carry a little extra weight on behalf of the non-music readers in the congregation when singing new hymns.

THE COMPLAINT

The church is a people. Most people have been given voices. Unfortunately they don't always use them only to sing. Some feel the calling to be the spokesperson for the mythical myriad (who without a doubt feel the same way that they do) in letting the church musician know the error of his/her ways!

When you receive complaints about your decisions or practices, it is important to listen. There may be an important point for you to hear! Sometimes it may be direct and clear: "We didn't know when the introduction was done!" Sometimes the problem may not be specifically what the person is saying, but be related to what is really the issue. For example, after one service a pastor told me one of the hymns was too fast. I thought, "No way. I remember. It was just right." I thanked him for letting me know, and listened to the tape of the service to see if he was right. The tempo was OK, but I was cutting each breath a bit short, so the congregation felt as though they had a boot in the backside as each phrase began: they felt pushed. The tempo wasn't too fast, but the breathing was too short. It was a very important thing to be brought to my attention, but merely slowing down would not have helped.

When someone complains about having to "keep track of all those fancy instructions for each stanza—can't we just sing a hymn?" One defensive response could be, "Fine, have your blah-ness." A better response could be to see if the bulletin instructions are clear.

Remember that if your practice represents change, be patient. People may grumble, but without change there is no life, and ultimately people know it. They may not yet see the large picture. In time they will understand. You can, however, moderate your pace of change.

It is also possible that the person's complaint has absolutely nothing to do with you or the church. I have had the experience of attempting to react to criticism only to find out there was something going on in the criticizer's life that had nothing to do with me or the church. It could be that a home or work situation is making someone feel so powerless that they try to exert control somewhere. Why not at church? There is absolutely nothing you can do in this situation except love that person all the more, pray for the person, and recognize that it is not about you.

When dealing with complaints it is important to take two steps backward and ask yourself the following questions:

- Are they right? (Could be...)
- Is there something behind this specific complaint that warrants action?
- Is this a large-picture issue requiring simple patience?
- Could this be projection of something totally unrelated?

Actually, I don't mind complaints. They can be a teaching moment, either for me or for the person issuing the complaint. I love to talk one-on-one with people about why we did something the way we did. Usually they'll say, "Oh. No one has explained that to me." Sometimes, I learn that I must change. In either case, after personal discussion, growth has occurred. Invariably a strengthened relationship and increased trust results.

HELP! I'M A PIANIST DRAFTED TO PLAY THE ORGAN!

Relax. You can indeed do this! There are incredible similarities between piano and organ. Enjoy *them*. You still use fingers on a keyboard, and the music uses grand staff with treble and bass clefs. Good start, eh?

Here are some things to remember in differentiating the two:

- The organ keyboard does not respond to how hard or lightly you play. Loud and soft is achieved through registration. (See Chapter 3.) The touch can be lighter (still with great control), with less of your body involved.

- There is no sustain pedal and the sound does not decay as you hold down the key. You will need to get used to keeping the keys depressed for full note values instead of achieving the full note value with your right foot on the sustain pedal with the piano! This may have an effect on your fingering as well. Tricks such as finger substitutions become more needed on the organ (changing from second finger to thumb while a note is depressed). Accents are accomplished through articulation—how much space is before and after a note—rather than by pressing the key harder.

- YOU DO NOT HAVE TO PLAY THE PEDAL! Putting these lower limbs into the mix can be terribly frightening. Add pedals gradually. It is OK to leave them out initially. After a while, add the two final notes of the hymn (usually V-I) when you are comfortable with the manuals. After six months of doing that, add other cadence points.

- If you can eventually add the pedal, don't work harder than you have to by doubling the bass line with your left hand and pedal. Get used to not playing the bass line on the manual. This is harder at first, but easier later.

- Practice ON THE ORGAN, not the piano. In other words, don't practice all week at home on the piano and expect to come to the church on Sunday and do well on the organ. The touch, the feel, and the sound are different. You must practice on that instrument itself in the worship space itself. Don't underestimate the difficulty of changing stops between stanzas. Practice this as well. It's the choreography of organ playing.

◆ You can concentrate on the octaves closest to middle C. You do not need to play octaves in either hand. The stops on the organ do those things for you. (This is why the keyboard can be shorter.)

Using octaves in both hands produces a full sound with the piano:

On the organ, this is all you need. Other octaves are accomplished by the stops on the organ:

It's also less work!

Example 6.1. "Praise to the Lord," Tune: LOBE DEN HERREN, *Ernewertes Gesangbuch*, Stralsund, 1665.

Like anything in life, you will find playing the organ easier the more you do it. Practice as much as you can *on the organ*, and do not assume it to be just like piano. There is enough literature for organ music without pedals that you needn't panic about the *pain of de feet.*

WHAT TO GET FIRST?

Pipes, piano, or else?

It is an unfortunate assumption that all churches need an organ. What the church needs is the song. The question needs to be, "What do we need for the hymn or song to happen?"

It is true that one of the most effective instruments for leading communal song is the pipe organ, for many reasons mentioned earlier. It is a "vocal" instrument like the human voice, creating sound with vibration caused by air going through a tube. It can lead larger gatherings without electronic amplification; it can lead the fullest praise; it can evoke the quietest prayer. It produces a great variety of sounds all through one person: the organist.

And it is true that most of our church songs are best led with organ. I believe that will continue to be the case even as we add new kinds of songs that are not best led with organ. It has survived hundreds of years as the church's main instrument, and I believe will go hundreds more. I also believe it to be a great gift and asset that the organ is indeed unique to the church, generally not a part of the secular culture. It is set-aside for the special purpose of drawing us into the holy—drawing us into song.

Yet, pipe organs are indeed expensive.

Ideally, for a church I would recommend a good pipe organ and a good piano. Many churches who say they can't *can* afford both. They only need to decide that their song is important enough. Sometimes high-quality electronic organs with advanced technology are considered. Perhaps they are a sensible way to go. However, it could be that a smaller pipe organ could have the same cost (and last quite a bit longer) than a larger quality electronic organ. I'd rather hold out for the real thing, the true acoustic tone production of a pipe organ. True vibration as opposed to synthetically produced vibration may be much different from what we scientifically know at this point. Silk flowers can look like the real thing, but what of the aroma?

Some churches, however, truly cannot afford a pipe organ. In this case it would be better to find a good piano, or sing unaccompanied with the help of a small group of singers singing from behind or among the people, or use instrumentalists in the congregation rather than just get an old rejected electronic house organ.

In any of these cases, the best help the congregation can be provided with would be good acoustics. That is, live acoustics with reverberation. In good acoustics the worshipers hear the entire gathering of people singing instead of only themselves.

A suggested plan for young churches where everything cannot be done at once:

- ◆ 1. Provide good acoustics. (Rip out carpet, pew pads, "acoustic tile" ceilings, and use hard gloss paint.)
- ◆ 2. Organize a group of singers and instrumentalists to lead the singing. (Lead vocally not visually. Visual leadership sets up a dependence, and in some cases replaces the people's song. A group of singers can lead from behind or among the people for the best vocal leadership.)
- ◆ 3. Get a piano—a good one. A good piano is a valuable investment. A bad piano is a waste.
- ◆ 4. Get a pipe organ.
- ◆ 5. Get percussion instruments (conga drums, clavés, guiros, shakers, large drums).

Then, depending upon where you are in this sequence, it makes sense to find printed worship and song materials that are best served with your musical resources. If piano is your main helpmate, liturgy settings and hymns that are pianistic (or unaccompanied) would work best. Music by Marty Haugen, for example works best with piano and not organ.

CONCLUSION

Clarity, variety, preparation, thoughtfulness and meaning—with these how can people resist? How can they keep from singing?

Experience says that great effort puts forth great results. If we put great effort into preparing for the ever-so-important songs, there will be response. If we don't...

The first half of the book has dealt with basics and some starting ideas. Now let's talk about long-term abilities: learning to improvise!

Part II:

SERIOUSLY IMPROVISING...

Getting Beyond the Notes on the Page....

INTRODUCTION

In the United States and Canada organists and pianists generally obtain their training through the learning of previously composed literature. The musicians learn how to read music from the page, and through these compositions technique is sharpened. But, classical music training on this continent is one of the few musical venues in the world in which learning improvisation is not a major component! Many musical styles, including jazz, rock, and pop, do not include much note reading at all. The music of African, Native American, Hispanic, and other cultures demand abilities in improvisation.

Yet here in our part of the world (North America), for church musicians, it is assumed that one needs to be born with special sparklies in order to "have the gift", and that, if one cannot improvise an organ symphony when given a theme at a recital, it can't be done.

Improvisation is a learned ability, a language. Acquiring the ability is just like learning to type on a typewriter or computer keyboard or like learning another spoken language. It is a craft that is indeed learnable by anyone. Not all will become like Paul Manz or Marcel Dupré, but anyone can learn to change one chord, or perhaps even learn how to harmonize a melody. It does not happen overnight, I'm sorry to report. It does take the "P" word (Practice). Like anything else, the more it is done, and the more it is actually practiced, the easier it will get. Bach himself said "Anyone can improvise like I do. All they have to do is practice."

In Germany I had two organ teachers: one for literature and one for improvisation. I had to practice equally for each. The demands were high for each. German church musicians had to be able to harmonize a hymn tune several different ways at sight, improvise a number of forms: bicinium, trio, fugue, toccata, passacaglia, and more. This improvisation is not considered a gift, but rather one of the many skill and knowledge requirements of the church musician.

This is not Germany, however, and these requirements do not exist for organists in our part of the world. In fact, in some situations, churches feel lucky to find anyone with a tiny bit of training in playing at all. Some organists feel good if they can just get through a hymn without ulcers, let alone add any improvisation. And for those with good training it is indeed possible to do a great job without developing the ability to improvise. In both cases, though, we are totally dependent upon the composers and publishers to provide us with what we need to accomplish all that I have discussed in Part One of this book. How can they know our people? The abilities of the accompanist? The worship space? The instrument?

Trusting "the force"[1] alone, hoping something cool will happen is also not enough. While this section of the book seems only to apply to organists and Western classical music, it is appropriate for anyone who accompanies congregational singing, regardless of style. The abilities outlined in this book are equally liberating to modern styles—jazz, rock and pop as well as classical. Harmony, counterpoint, and form are a vital part of percussion-based music, and learning these foundations will lead to further freedom. If rock musicians studied harmony and counterpoint

[1]A spiritual source of intuition and guidance referred to in the movie series, "Star Wars."

there would be even more interesting progressions and tunes. If drummers studied counterpoint, more options could open up for them. African drums produce counterpoint, avoiding duplication—simply looking for "the spaces to fill." With knowledge of harmony, counterpoint and form, we can see possibilities as well as feel them, and then make them happen.

Many of the piano styles mentioned in Part One of this book would be greatly helped if the skills in this part of the book are developed first. Playing Black-Gospel piano is much more imaginable when one can see how harmonies and applied harmonies work together to form and embellish a harmonic pattern.

The abilities covered in this section are NOT for classical organists and pianists only.

Learning to improvise takes time and effort, but is very freeing, allowing us to custom tailor what we do to the moment, context, and people, without a large budget. It also develops more balanced musicians by bridging the left and right brain hemispheres.[2]

Many people tend to favor their left brains and think they are incapable of improvisation. They cannot "see" harmonies except when printed on the page. Some people are primarily right brained, and for them to play literature is quite a chore and frightening. They'd rather make it up. For these people, harmonies happen. Their fingers stumble upon them. Sometimes they stop to figure out what a chord is, but usually just enjoy what happens by chance.

Medical science proves that we all can utilize both brain hemispheres. We tend to favor one of the two. Yet when we work at engaging and developing both together we strengthen each. Fully developed musicianship is a healthy combination of the technical-mechanical (left brain) and the full enjoyment of the art (right brain). Improvisation is not exclusively a right-brain activity. Through the process provided here, you will begin to analytically see harmonies coming by noting melody notes and being able to imagine what the harmonic possibilities are with these melody notes. You can see the pitch "G" coming at the end of a phrase and imagine an E-minor chord instead of the printed G major. But the connection of both brain halves takes work.

In this section of the book, I have outlined a process that you can do over time. Take plenty of it along the way! Take each step slowly and live with it for a while. Remember how many years it took you to learn to read and play compositions. The difference this time is that you already have the technical ability to play. You now need your imagination for the notes!

I begin with the very simple and move to the more complex. Keep this book by the keyboard and plug away at it over the next several years. Make these exercises the first 15 minutes of each practice session. Consider them along the same line that you did scales and arpeggios in the early piano years.

There are two dimensions to improvisation that we will explore in this section: harmony and counterpoint. An additional section goes beyond to form. Some of the steps for learning harmony and counterpoint can be simultaneously practiced, or may be done one at a time. The three sections are intertwined: what you learn in harmony is applied to counterpoint, and understanding counterpoint helps you understand construction of better alto or tenor lines (J. S. Bach's amazing ability). Then both are applied when creating form as the third section will demonstrate.

Again, go slowly; allow for time in each step.

---

[2]Referring to the scientific theories of the brain hemispheres: the right generally processes intuition and space; the left brain, logic and sequence

Chapter 7

HARMONY

GETTING STARTED

Any particular pitch has an enormous number of options for harmony that include that pitch itself. Each of these chords has a different effect or color on that pitch. Take the following "G" to the piano, and notice the different effect these harmonies have on the G:

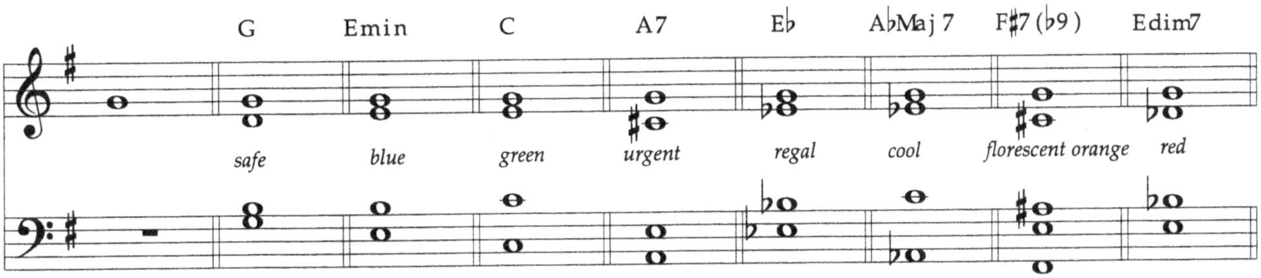

Example 7.1 The note "G" harmonized different ways.

Often when we see such a note, the only option we think of is G major. The above example shows that this is not the case at all.

➤ STEP 1: Begin to "see" other chords under pitches in hymnal settings.

A vital step is beginning to "see" other chords under pitches (in your imagination) rather than merely what's printed, or the chord of the note itself.

Write in at least 6 options for the following pitch D:

Example 7.2. Harmonizing the pitch "D".

Now let's apply this to hymnody itself. When we see a melody note "G" in a hymn, within a G major chord, we needn't assume that G major is the only option for that particular moment.

➤ STEP 2: Change one chord in the middle of a hymn.

In your early improvisation career, consider changing one chord in a hymn. Not a dramatic change, one that mostly musicians might notice. Sometimes the text itself suggests a chord change. For example:

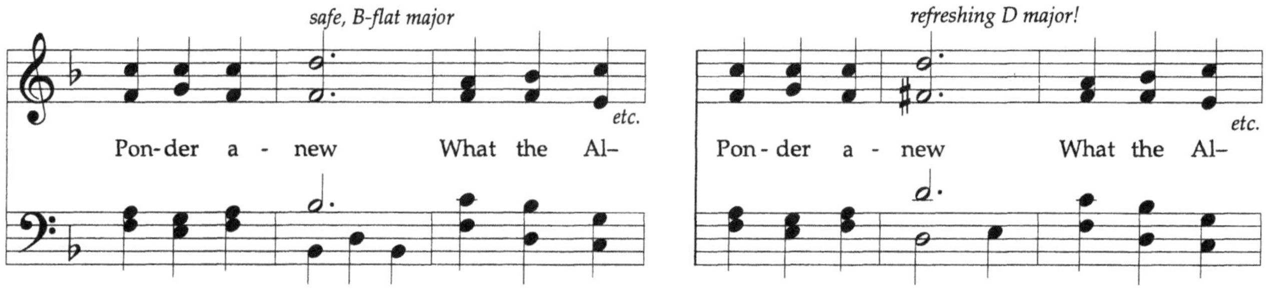

Example 7.3. "Praise to the Lord, the Almighty," Stanza 3, phrase 3. Text: Joachim Neander, 1650–80; tr. Catherine Winkworth, 1829–78. Tune: LOBE DEN HERREN, *Erneuertes Gesangbuch*, Stralsund, 1665.

With the following examples, imagine at least two or three options for the chords left blank with these familiar hymns:

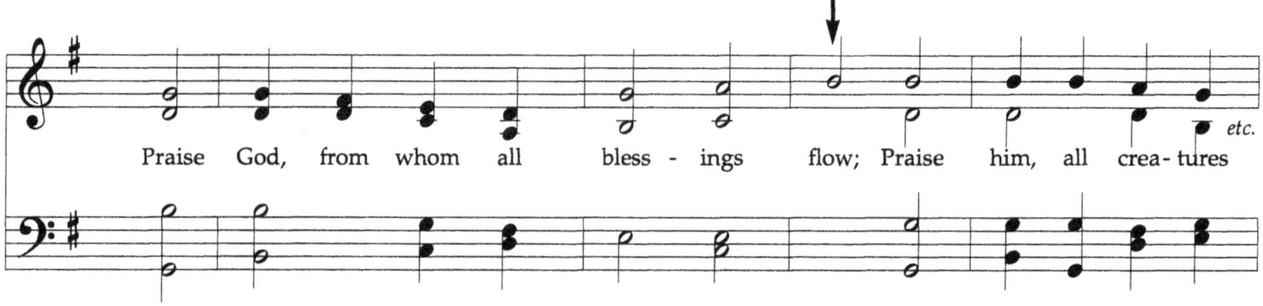

Example 7.4. "Praise God, from Whom All Blessings Flow," Text, Thomas Ken, 1637–1711. Tune: OLD HUNDREDTH, Louis Bourgeois, c. 1510-c. 1561.

Example 7.5. "Oh, Worship the King," Text: Robert Grant, 1779–1838. Tune: HANOVER, William Croft, 1678–1727.

Select a hymn on your own and look at the ending notes for each phrase. Divorcing yourself from the printed harmony for that note, imagine a different chord for one of these phrases. Is there another chord that could be used within the same key of the hymn? Be careful not to use chords that draw people away from subsequent melody notes. At this point, figure this out by ear. Try continuing on the melody after your new chord. If it works, it is probably OK.

The next example, 7.6, is an example of a chord detracting from a subsequent note of the melody. The "F major" chord makes us want to sing B-flat soon after, not B-natural. (We all know that the best advice is to "B-natural!")

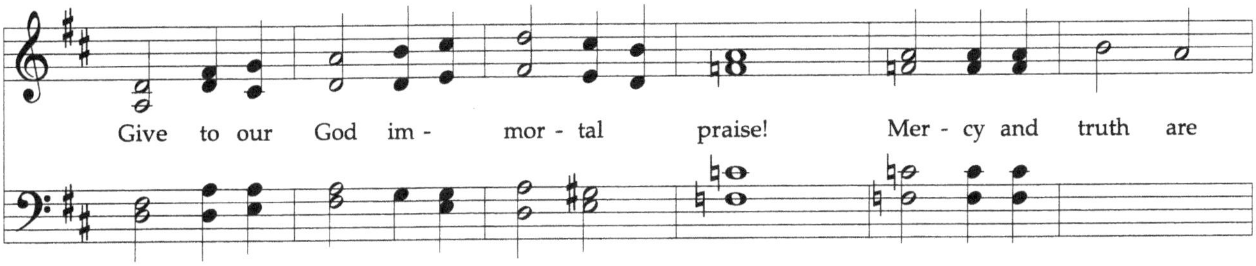

Example 7.6. "Give to Our God Immortal Praise!" Text: Isaac Watts, 1674–1738.
Tune: DUKE STREET, attr. John Hatton, d. 1793.

So perhaps this is how you get started. Change one chord, only one. Then go back to the printed harmonies in the book because you will be so nervous. Next year, do it again with another hymn. After six months, change two chords in one service. Then three, then . . .

APPLIED DOMINANTS

The accidental in the following example is announcing something very significant:

Example 7.7. "Give to Our God Immortal Praise!" Text: Isaac Watts, 1674–1738.
Tune: DUKE STREET, attr. John Hatton, d. 1793.

Most accidentals in hymn settings are part of a wonderful event in a hymn's harmony. The chord containing the accidental is taking the hymn out of the land of its original key. The "new key" may be for two chords, but a new key is explored briefly. Any chord can be strengthened by its preceding chord, especially if it is its "dominant" chord.

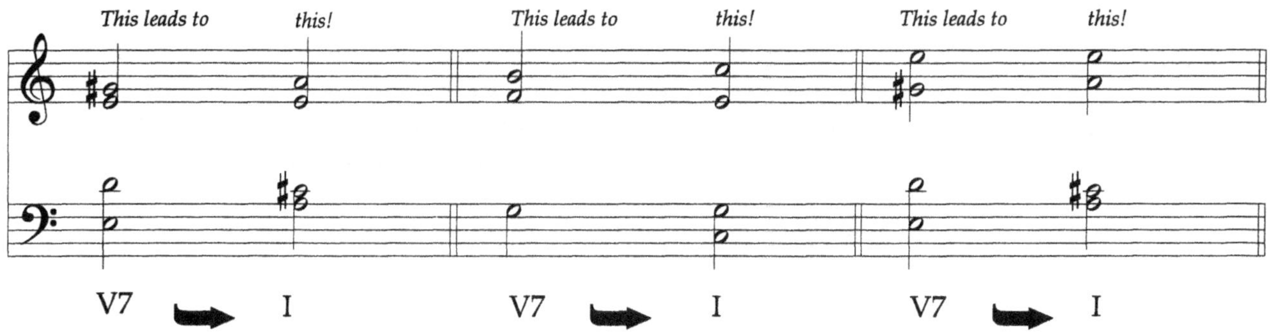

Example 7.8. Examples of applied dominants.

Using applied dominant chords as demonstrated in example 7.8 creates one of the strongest harmonic progressions: V7-I.

In the case of "Give to Our God Immortal Praise!" the last note of the first phrase is "A" printed with an A major chord. The A major chord on the word "praise" is strengthened by its dominant chord: E major.

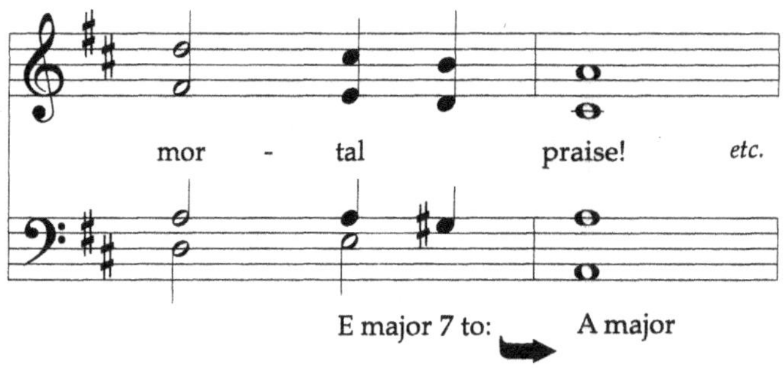

Example 7.9. from "Give to Our God Immortal Praise!" DUKE STREET.

What makes E major stick out like a rush of mint, is the note G-sharp. G-sharp is NOT A PART OF THE KEY OF this hymn (D major). So, for a blink of an eye, we leave the land of D major to strengthen the A major chord.

The E major 7 chord **applies** to the A major chord.

➤ STEP 3: Change TWO chords in a hymn, the first of them being an applied dominant chord.

Above we discussed changing ONE chord in a hymn. Now begin seeing if you can strengthen your new chord with a chord that applies to it. For example, the same phrase analyzed above could end with F-sharp minor instead of A major.

Example 7.10. "Give to Our God Immortal Praise!" DUKE STREET. A different chord for the end of the first phrase.

The dominant chord of F-sharp minor would be C-sharp major with or without a seventh (B-natural). Looking at the melody notes that precede the note "A" of the word, "praise," I find C-sharp, and B-natural which can allow the applied dominant C-sharp and passing seventh of B-natural leading to F-sharp minor. Here's what that looks (and sounds like):

Example 7.11. "Give to Our God Immortal Praise!" DUKE STREET. An "applied" dominant added.

The E-sharp could be eliminated and an acceptable progression would remain. But the E-sharp creates an applied chord (C-sharp major) which strongly announces the F-sharp chord which immediately follows it. And, it is a breath of fresh air in the vast land of D major.

Perhaps by now you can begin to activate your imagination and connect the imagination to your fingers. Can you see several "applied dominant" possibilities in the following ending phrase of the tune DARWALL'S 148TH? I've provided some arrows to hint at some possibilities. Begin with a chord under an arrow . What harmony could be under this note? Does the melody note immediately preceding this note allow an applied dominant which would include a pitch not in the key signature (i.e., one that would require an accidental)?

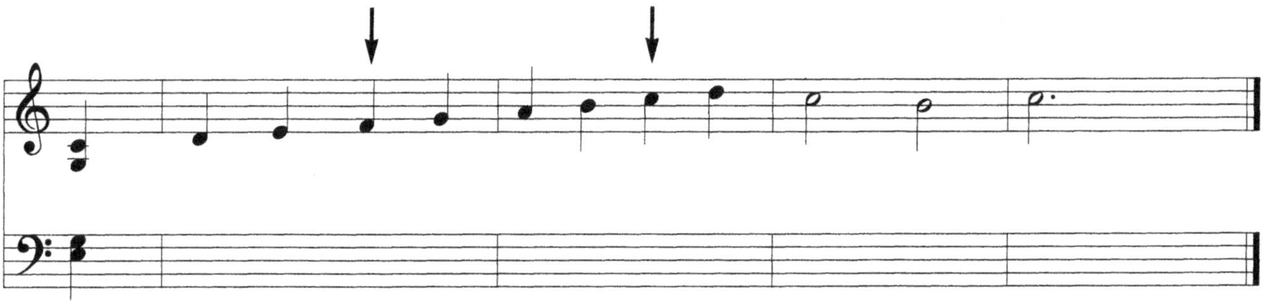

Example 7.12. The last line from the tune DARWALL'S 148TH, by John Darwall, 1731–89.

Try some other familiar hymns. If your eyes are opened to this possibility, you should be ready to move on.

WARNING! Excessive use of applied dominants may cause rolling of the eyes on the part of the trained musicians in your parish.

Applied dominants can be overused, like most things in this book. Save them for good moments. Ascending to a high melody note would be a good moment. But not every stanza, every hymn, every week. Too much. When used too much they have no power.

➤ STEP 4: Harmonize "Amen" many different ways

Since "Amen" means "so be it", you may indeed wish different chords to emphasize that which everyone is "amen-ing." Complete some possibilities above. Imagine when you might use them. Perhaps there are other very short liturgical sentences or words sung in your services. See if you can find some alternative harmonies for them (in your practicing—not in the service itself.) At this point, do not worry yet about how many notes you play simultaneously. Just play chords.

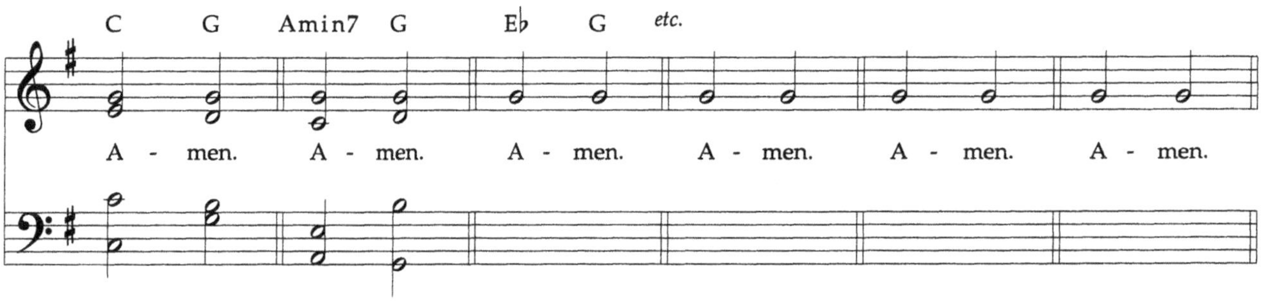

Example 7.13. "Amen."

After changing one or two chords from time to time, begin working on harmonizing longer melodies.

LEARNING TO HARMONIZE MELODIES—

Do we have to follow the rules?

Perhaps not initially. It may be enough just to be able to put harmonies under a tune without worrying about how many fingers you have on the keyboard. However, it is helpful to be able to think in terms of traditional western harmony.

Some introductory information first. There are seven pitches used in a typical major scale:

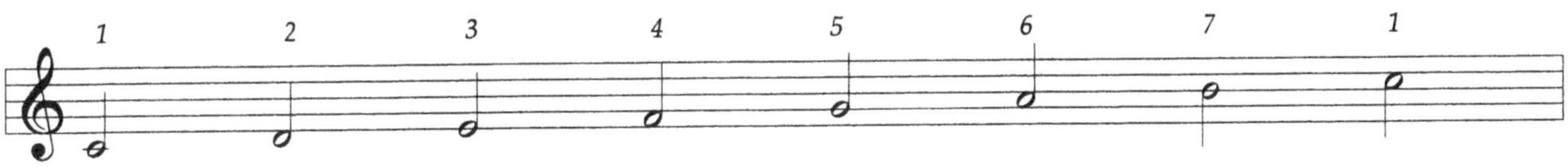

Example 7.14. The C major scale.

When we use the word "harmony," we are referring to when two or more notes are sounding together. Some combinations of these notes are easier to listen to than others. Remember that music is vibration: Each individual pitch in itself is actually a combination of pitches vibrating together, called the *harmonic series.* That means that each pitch itself includes:

Example 7.15. The harmonic series. (An X-ray of the vibration of an individual pitch.)

If you went to the organ and played a 16′ Subbass low note, you would be able to hear the note an octave and a fifth above that note as a part of the pitch. That is the harmonic series in a range where the individual component pitches of the series can be heard. The first few pitches of a series vibrate with greater ease. They are the foundational pitches, which is what our ears mainly hear. Notes that sound in harmony to each other are usually those that are in these lower pitches of the series: the octave and the fifth. The next interval in the series is the third. Harmony of the octave and fifth almost sound like the pitch itself, because in a way they are! This also explains why in early chant, the first "harmony" was singing at a fifth parallel to the melody of the chant. It really was another way of singing in unison.

The clearest harmony notes tend to be the third and the fifth, the triad.

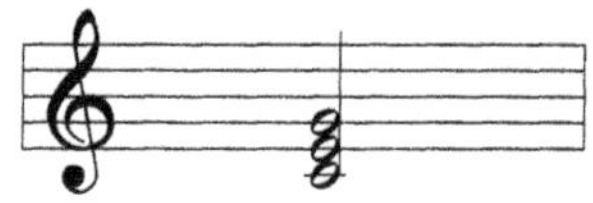

Example 7.16. The triad, made up of the third and the fifth.

In modern harmony, the other pitches of the scale are also used often. The seventh, being very powerful, is discussed later. But primarily, the root, third and fifth are used for clear harmony.

Example 7.17. The third and fifth are used for building the triad.

In any key, there are three primary chords that together include all the notes of the scale.

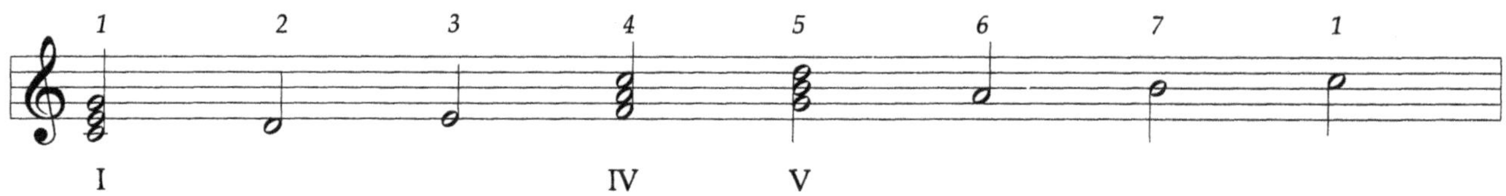

Example 7.18. Primary chords. Roman numerals indicate on which note of the scale a harmonic triad is built. These three triads together include all seven notes of the scale.

When harmonizing a melody, how we place these triad notes together with a melody note is our task. How many notes should be used, and where do we place them to form strong and consequential harmony? Over time some guidelines and "rules" have developed, and for good reasons.

Play the following two examples:

Example 7.19. LIEBSTER JESU. Two progressions:
Number one not observing harmonic rules, number two following them.

At this point, it may be that you are not able to hear the difference, but the first simply has too many notes. In the second example, the harmony and voice-leading structures are much easier to "see"—an important part of this process. It is hard to see the beautiful flowers in the garden when the weeds are too plentiful. Once you have trained your eyes, you will look at good hymnal settings and notice that most chords have two root notes, one third and one fifth. The root note is most often doubled, giving the root a stronger sound. Then you can understand why that particular chord is stronger, and why the way the pitches of the chord are placed leads the ear easily into the next chord. By seeing, you can direct your fingers more efficiently to good harmonies. While the untrained ear may indeed not notice the difference between good voicing and weak voicing, it is there. It is your job to train your ears on their behalf, and then tell your fingers where to go!

THINK VOCALLY

In theoretical terms, a typical hymn is prepared in four-voice harmonization, and you will hear the word "voicing." Indeed, we must think *vocally* in every respect. Would you have your altos sing an alto line that stays above C above middle C? Would there be a revolt if the tenor line is simply too boring? Even though you are playing the keyboard, think in terms of soprano, alto, tenor, and bass. When you work with only four notes at a time, seeing easily what's being played, you also begin to learn about *how* the inner notes of harmony work consequentially from chord to chord, and how the inner notes help one chord lead to the next. We'll come back to what to avoid and why in a bit.

Four-voice harmony is indeed a language. Alto lines tend to flow a certain way, as do tenor and bass lines. Let's see how they work.

➤ STEP 5: Play a hymn from the hymnal, and sing the alto line. Then the tenor. Then the bass.

At first, it is okay to play the same part you are singing, but then move to NOT playing the voice you are singing, letting your voice complete the harmony. This will assist you in physically feeling how these voices work in harmonizing. Do this a lot. You will be amazed at how similar these voices begin to sound from hymn to hymn. This is correct. There is a language to these parts that happens naturally.

Next, harmonize a tune that you know so well, you won't have to think too hard about it and can focus entirely on your harmonization work: the scale!

➤ STEP 6: Harmonize the scale, using four-voice harmonization.

Example 7.20. C major scale harmonized with the three primary chords.

Begin with D major, harmonizing only with the three primary chords (I-D major, IV-G major, and V-A major). As mentioned earlier, these three chords include all the notes of the scale.

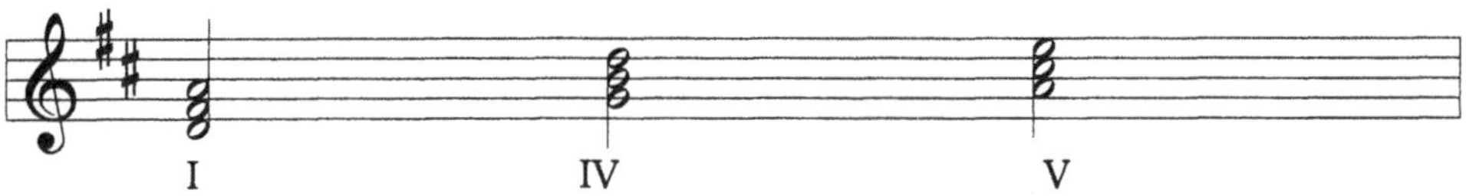

Example 7.21. The three primary chords for D major.

Then, in like manner, harmonize the A major scale, E major, B major, B-flat major, E-flat major. These keys with their sharps and/or flats assist you in remaining oriented on the keyboard, rather than dealing with all white notes. (I have provided C major in the above example because this will NOT be your first scale, so you can't just cheat and play what I have provided as the example!) After mastering the major scales using the three main harmonies, add more chords—perhaps even including applied dominants as demonstrated in step 3. Then try minor scales. C minor, F minor, E minor, etc. Do not use chords with the seventh yet. The seventh is very powerful, and we'll get to it later.

Example 7.22. The F major scale harmonized using many chords, including some applied dominants.

Back to the rules: They are as follows, along with the logic to them in italics:

- ◆ 1. Use only four voices: soprano and alto in the treble clef played with the right hand; tenor in the bass clef played with the left hand; bass in the bass clef played with the feet. (Or if you are adventurous, get used to playing the tenor and alto with the left hand, and the soprano only with the right hand.) Keep the voices within an octave of each other except bass and tenor which can be separated by as much as an octave and a half.

  Logic: You are thinking vocally, remember? Soprano, alto, tenor, and bass. Spacing them within an octave keeps you in good singing ranges and retains the clearest sound. Higher and lower sounds than this range are achieved through organ registration. Basically, stay on the grand staff.

Example 7.23. Examples of good spacing, bad spacing.

- ◆ 2. Double the root or in some cases the third of a chord. Try not to double the fifth. The chord is strongest when the root is doubled. Let your ear inform you. Play the following and notice the "weaker" chords.

  Logic: As mentioned earlier, mainly the triad is used: three notes. Yet we have four voices. One note of the triad will be used twice when constructing basic harmony. Proper doubling keeps harmony and voice-leading clear: what is this chord? The root (or octave) and third are the clearest indicators. Doubling the fifth creates a feeling of a false root—more like a final cadence (in theory terms, cadential six-four chord).

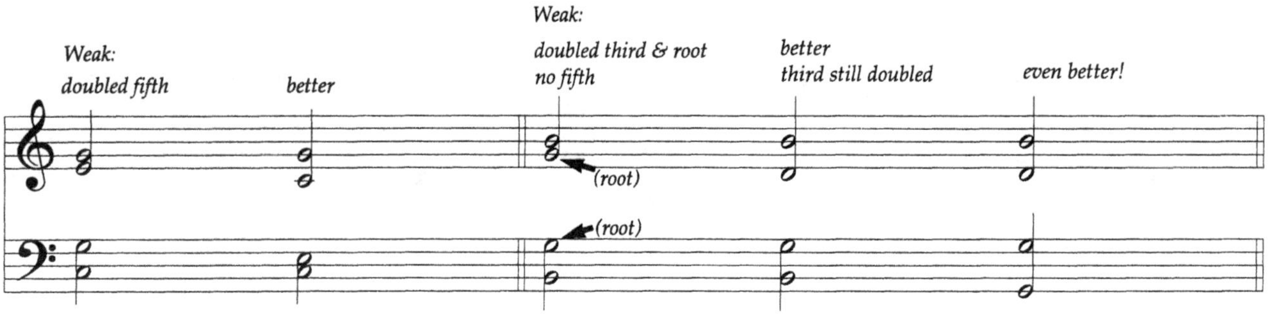

Example 7.24. Examples of doubling.

◆ 3. Strive to have the root in the bass (pedal), or in some cases the third. Avoid putting the fifth in the bass. It sounds weak, or like a cadence (which may be your desire, but avoid it for now).

Logic: Can you imagine a wooden house with a concrete attic? It would not seem very stable. The strength of the foundation needs to be lower in most cases.

Example 7.25. Bass note with fifth (weak), then third (better), then root (best).

◆ 4. Avoid two voices moving together in unison or fifths or octaves.

Logic: They no longer sound like two independent voices. They sound like one. It would be as if the sopranos disappeared for a chord. Unison and the fifth are the first two pitches in the harmonic series. Every pitch includes these two in their lowest vibrational make-up: the harmonic series.

Example 7.26. Voices moving together in parallel octaves and fifths.

◆ 5. Try not to have all voices move in the same direction. At least one voice should move in an opposing direction, or remain on the same pitch.

Logic: Often when all the voices move in the same direction, it may be caused by not following rules 3 and 4 above.

Example 7.27. Examples of similar motion, then contrary motion. By starting the bass up an octave in the second example, there is room to go down as the melody goes up.

Now go back to harmonizing the scales and think about these things as you go. You may need to go very slowly, perhaps stopping and holding each chord as you figure out the next one. This is okay! It will become faster the more you do it, and, as with singing inner parts, eventually the harmonizations begin to sound the same. It is this eventual boredom with what you figure out that will drive you to search for more interesting harmonies.

➤ STEP 7: Harmonize familiar tunes.

Write out only the melody (so you don't spoil the effort by cheating in reading the printed harmonies) and harmonize. Go as slowly as you need. Do not worry if you think you are merely coming up with what you remember in the hymn book. This is all right, because you are still going through the process of seeing the note on the page, and seeing harmonies under it, and spelling out that harmony using your brain and fingers together.

➤ STEP 8: Harmonize unfamiliar tunes.

➤ STEP 9: Play the melody with the right hand; the alto and tenor with the left hand.

This frees you to solo out the melody on another keyboard if you wish. It may feel awkward at first, but in time you will get used to it. Besides freeing the right hand to solo out the melody, this also keeps the distance between alto and tenor within an octave. However, be careful about not getting too great a distance between soprano and alto.

Example 7.28. Tune: WAS GOTT TUT DAS IST WOHLGETAN, attr. Severus Gastorius, c. 1650–c. 1693.

If you are this far in your practicing, it has probably been about two years. Good progress. Let's get frisky.

➤ STEP 10: Play the melody in the left hand, harmonize with the soprano and alto in the right hand.

Still observe the guidelines and rules listed above.

Example 7.29. Example of the melody in the "tenor," "Evening and Morning," Tune: DIE GÜLDNE SONNE, Johann G. Ebeling, 1637–76.

➤ STEP 11: Play the melody in the pedal; put the harmony above.

Considering the rule that the pedal should play either the root or third, this can be a challenge. Work through it slowly. If things are going well, you may even notice a nice descant happening in the soprano.

Example 7.30. Melody in the pedal. "Savior of the Nations, Come," Tune: NUN KOMM, DER HEIDEN HEILAND, J. Walther, *Geystliche gesangk Buchleyn*, 1524.

SEVENTH CHORDS,
and the pulls of nature

At this point you are allowed to add some seventh chords, especially in final cadences.

Example 7.31. The last phrase of "Now Thank We All Our God,"
Tune: NUN DANKET ALLE GOTT, Johann Crüger, 1598–1662.

The seventh is a very powerful tone. Its gravitational pulls are extremely strong. It is usually used in the dominant chord (V7) leading to its tonic (I) for which there would not need to be an accidental. We all know the effect of someone playing a rousing dominant seventh chord, and walking away from the piano. It drives us crazy. We need to hear it resolve!

The dominant seventh needs to resolve the seventh down a half step (to become the third of the final chord).

Example 7.32. The resolution of the seventh.

Related to this is the seventh degree of a scale. In C major it is B-natural.

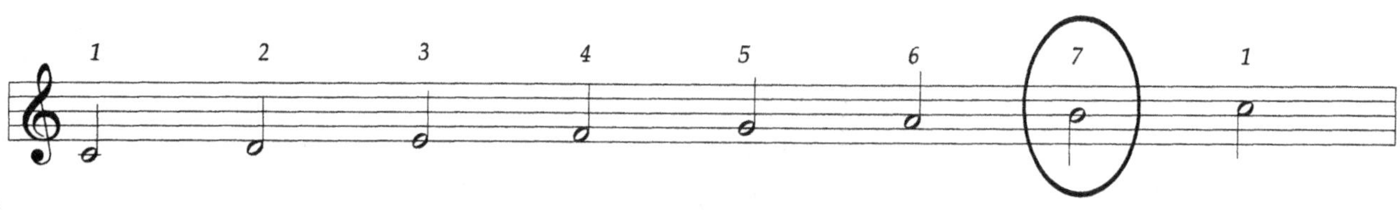

Example 7.33. The C major scale, seventh circled.

When this degree of the scale is used either in a melody or in harmony, it too has strong gravity: it wants to resolve up a half-step, to home-base tonic. It has the nickname "leading tone" because it leads to home.

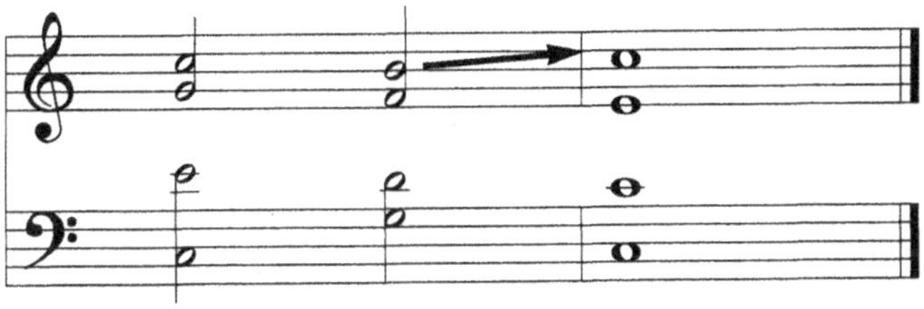

Example 7.34. "B" as melody note, resolving to "C". When this note is used in harmony, it often is the third of a dominant chord.

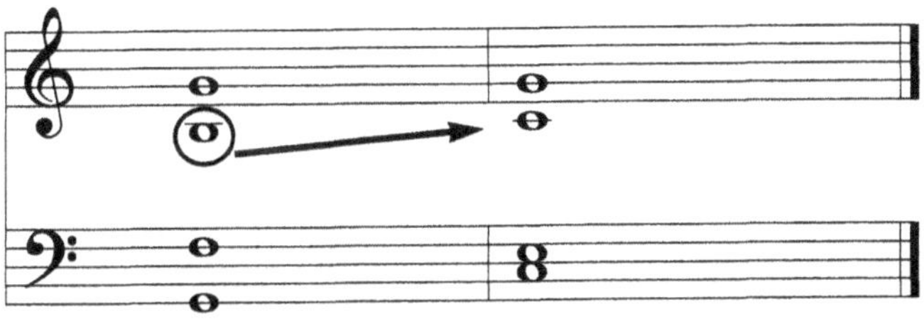

Example 7.35. "B" as the third of a dominant G7 chord. It resolves to "C".

Given the leading tone's strong pulls, it is also a good reason not to double the third. Can you guess why? (It would create parallel octaves if both resolve up as gravity suggests.)

When combined with a dominant seventh chord, the third wants to resolve up a half step, and the seventh down a half step. Play both of the following examples, one where this resolution does not happen, and one which correctly resolves these two notes:

Example 7.36. Resolutions of the third and seventh.

In the first example of 7.36, it is noticeable to the ear that something is wrong. You, having just acquired this information, can scientifically explain why the adrenaline level of the human body has been increased by a bad resolution of the third and seventh.

WARNING! The use of seventh chords is powerful, and the improper resolution of the third and seventh therein may cause hiccups.

Knowledge of the seventh informs you about chords you can or cannot use. For example, using a seventh chord when the melody note itself is the seventh is fine as long as the next note of the melody is a half step down.

Example 7.37. "Salvation unto Us Has Come," with C-natural resolving, then bad example.
Tune: ES IST DAS HEIL, *Etlich Christlich lider*, Wittenberg, 1524.

The seventh of a chord is powerful when playing the melody in the bass. Two of the ways a seventh chord can be effectively used with bass melody is when the seventh of the chord is the melody note itself, or in a final cadence where the melody moves from the second degree of the scale to one. In order to get a V7 to I cadence, it is possible to put the fifth in the bass, resolving to tonic. The following example shows both:

Example 7.38. The last phrase of "A Mighty Fortress Is Our God," melody in the pedal making use of seventh chords.
Tune: EIN FESTE BURG, Martin Luther, 1483–1546.

Whenever I see a melody descending by a half step, I imagine that I can use the first note of the descending half-step as the seventh when I am playing the melody in the pedal.

Seventh chords should be used with moderation, given their strong power. Like most things, if used too often, they are stripped of their power. (Are you beginning to catch a theme of moderation with all tricks taught in this book?!)

Bach understood the gravitational pulls of the seventh. He knew how to use the suspense of harmony to keep us on edge. He stretched the anticipated resolution of the seventh and third to physically keep our adrenaline pumping. If he had used the seventh chord too much, the suspense would have disappeared. Sounds our ears hear too consistently are screened out by our nervous system and no longer heard.

In our time, the use of the seventh is rampant.

Example 7.39. "Lord Keep Us Steadfast," harmonized with all seventh chords
Tune: ERHALT UNS, HERR, J. Klug, *Geistliche Lieder,* 1543.

Sounds like jazz, doesn't it? Sometimes this is the desired effect. I've noticed that Ray Charles sprinkles a flavor on everything he arranges. Analyzing what this "sprinkling" specifically is, I found that he adds a flatted seventh to just about every chord. Using the seventh chord all the time produces color alone, and when omnipresent it no longer provides strong gravitational pulls in the voices themselves.

Understanding this makes clear why rock music, which uses the seventh so frequently, has to resort to other techniques like rhythmic syncopation to supply the suspense. "Feeling the beat" in syncopation does indeed create a similar suspense to that of the seventh in harmony.

TRICKS TO DISCOVER MORE HARMONIC POSSIBILITIES

If you have gotten this far, congratulations! You are probably beginning to desire some new flavors to the language of four-voice harmony. Try the following in an effort to find something new:

- ◆ 1. Eliminate accidentals in inner voices. These are most likely applied harmonies (as described in step 3 earlier in this chapter), and the harmony will still work well without the accidental. Eliminating accidentals will usually lead to a "modal" sound.

- ◆ 2. Try making the melody the major third of a second-inversion chord. You might discover one chord you like and can use it sometime.

Example 7.40. "Praise to the Lord," with all six-four chords.
Tune: LOBE DEN HERREN, *Ernewertes Gesängbuch,* Stralsund, 1665.

- ◆ 3. Try harmonizing an entire hymn in its relative key. If in a major key, harmonize it in the relative minor.

Example 7.41. Stanza 3: "Blest Be the Tie That Binds,"
Tune: DENNIS, Johann G. Nägeli, 1773–1836. Text: John Fawcett, 1740–1817.

Or, if in a minor key, harmonize it in the relative major key:

Example 7.42. Stanza 4: "Let All Mortal Flesh Keep Silence," Tune: PICARDY, French folk tune, 17th century. Text: Liturgy of St. James; tr. Gerald Moultrie, 1829–85.

◆ 4. On occasions when the melody descends a whole step (especially in a cadence, like at the end of a phrase), consider a modal-style harmony for the first of those two notes. For example:

Example 7.43. Last phrase of "Love Divine All Loves Excelling," Tune: HYFRYDOL, Rowland H. Prichard, 1811–87.

Instead of the last two chords being C major to F, this example uses E-flat to F. Whenever I see a descending whole step, I consider this possibility. It is, however, a progression that I would use sparingly. It is very different, and using it too often would weaken it.

Learning to harmonize will be one of the greatest gifts you can unleash. From learning to harmonize you can branch out into many things that make singing for the congregation much more exciting. Like any gift, however, caution must be exercised! Harmony must always help the singer sing the melody and its text, not pull away from it. A little can go a long way.

Harmony is powerful. If you are doing it well, it would be subtle, not usually noticeable. What is not being espoused here is encouragement to see how wildly or differently you can harmonize a tune.

Example 7.44. "A Mighty Fortress Is Our God," very bizarre harmonization. Interesting, perhaps, but not helpful for congregation's singing.

Harmonies are a subtle way we can keep the congregation's vitality sustained in its song. Sometimes harmonization can bring out a text, or can make the singer feel boosted to sing a higher note, or can add suspense or can provide subtle variety. The ability to harmonize can also open doors in free improvisation, including hymn introductions, preludes and postludes.

In all cases, subtlety is the key. Music readers may notice. Many will not. Whether people consciously notice is not the point. Lifting up the song is. Re-harmonizing should not supercede the singing. If the congregation begins to sing the harmony they see in the book, your altered harmonization IS EXPENDABLE. Join them immediately!

Enough said. Now, let's look at more than one melody line working together, or counterpoint.

Chapter 8

COUNTERPOINT

It is easy to fall into the trap of thinking only vertically with music, especially when it comes to congregational song and hymnody. We think chord to chord. Earlier in the book I discussed how we need to consider chant horizontally; its linear motion from point "a" to "b" horizontally across the staff. We use the word *melody* to describe this line, but then tend to imply only the top note of the chords. What of the inner voices? The alto, tenor, and bass lines?

To go along with any given melody, we can create another simultaneous "melody" that sounds pleasing with the tune. This is called counterpoint: when one or more voices interact with the original tune, each in its own a lovely melody, yet each working in harmony with the tune.

Good counterpoint is that which is a healthy combination of vertical harmony and horizontal line. The ultimate master of counterpoint was J. S. Bach. His harmonizations of the chorales have set the standard that still remain unparalleled. Bach has composed loveable and singable alto lines and even interesting bass lines. Yet, horizontally, each chord is also masterfully crafted. The many compositions of J. S. Bach, the preludes and fugues, chorale preludes, and larger works are amazing displays of carefully-crafted counterpoint.

It is important to know about harmony. The previous chapter helps with that. But we can create harmony while making use of melodies to go with melodies. This can be in the form of two voices working together as if a flute player and an oboe were playing together, or it can be the four main vocal parts of a choir, or it can be a full orchestra of instruments.

Counterpoint is something I love to find in current compositions: a good balance of horizontal and vertical, rather than blobs of chords under a melody; inner lines that my alto section will like; inner lines that sing beautifully on the organ. One organ teacher I studied with had me sing the alto part of Bach pieces while playing the other parts. Then the tenor. Then the bass. An amazing understanding of the piece follows an exercise like that. Another teacher said "anyone can add some major sevenths to a familiar tune, and publish it for fat royalties." Ouch!

But what does this have to do with the typical organist and his or her task of helping the people sing?

WHERE WOULD COUNTERPOINT BE USED?

On a basic level, counterpoint may be applied to many situations. It may be used as a part of congregational song introductions, preludes, offertories, communion distribution music, and postludes. It can be used to create instrumental parts to accompany the congregational song. It can be used to write descants for hymns and choir settings of hymn stanzas. We can even use it to create alternative harmony for hymns. It can actually be a part of the skills I have discussed in Part One of this book.

Counterpoint is an important part of improvisation, and it, too, is very learnable. Below you will find another step-by-step list of exercises to develop the ability to improvise counterpoint. Again, these steps are simply mundane exercises created to develop a skill, not intended to create wonderful pieces every time you practice. The exercises may sound dull to you over time. Embrace that feeling. This boredom is what will drive you to venture into new risks!

GETTING STARTED

As with harmony, in counterpoint thinking is helpful. Using both halves of the brain is part of the process. However, when improvising counterpoint a big part of the process is letting go and trusting your fingers to simply go places. Now and then it works merely to think a harmony and see how your fingers play it. On occasion it helps to aim for a consonant interval on a strong beat when playing with two-voices. A consonant interval would most likely be unison, or intervals of a third, fourth, fifth, or sixth. Unison, thirds and sixths are especially good for this purpose. Fourths sound unfinished, and the fifths can sound empty.

TWO PARTS–for the beginner

Select a tune from the hymnal which is familiar to you. With your left hand on one manual and a light 8′ Reed or solo stop, play that melody only. With your right hand, play a line counter to the melody with 8′ and 2′ Flutes (or any color substantially different from the melody). This helps your brain sort out two distinct voices. As an exercise use steps 1-5 below for each hymn tune you select. Do it once a day with the same tune for a week. Then change tunes for the next week and do steps one through five again. Continue until you feel you are able to do this comfortably.

➤ STEP 1: In one hand, play the melody of a hymn. In the other, play a free melody, one note per beat.

Example 8.1. Tune: WAS GOTT TUT. attr. Severus Gastorius, c. 1650–c. 1693.

Some helpful hints:

- Play opposites. If the melody goes up, go down with your free voice.
- Don't get stuck in the same five-finger pattern area with the free voice—move up and around all over the keyboard. It is OK to cross over or under the melody. Think as if you have two different instruments—a flute and an oboe. If you get stuck, arpeggiate or jump an octave to get out.

◆ Rests can also be used in the free voice, especially on the downbeat.

Example 8.2. Tune: WAS GOTT TUT. attr. Severus Gastorius, c. 1650–c. 1693, using a rest in the free voice.

◆ Work with goal points such as strong beats or ending notes of a phrase. Start with a consonant interval such as an octave, then aim for arriving at a sixth at the ending note of the phrase. Don't worry about what's between. Just go there.

◆ Try not to stop! Even if you have a complete train wreck, it is good to learn how to recover from a wreck. If you cannot go on, start over. Slow down if necessary, but do not teach yourself to stop when you encounter a bump in the road. Just say to yourself that for a moment you are experimenting with contemporary/classical music. Aim for a consonant interval and move there.

◆ Remember that the goal is not a masterwork each time you practice. The goal is to get used to doing it, and, from time to time, to discover some moves that you like, repeating these. It is by going over and over this process that the improvisation gets better. Each time through you shave a bit more mud off. As you go over and over it, you get closer to the jewel hidden inside.

◆ You may make use of patterns, particularly in steps 2 through 5. But do not get stuck with one pattern. Use variety. A pattern should not continue more than a measure.

Example 8.3. Overuse of a pattern.

➤ STEP 2: Using the same melody, play eighth notes with the free-voice.

Example 8.4. Tune: WAS GOTT TUT, attr. Severus Gastorius, c. 1650–c. 1693.
Melody in left hand, right hand free with eighth notes.

➤ STEP 3: Same melody, play triplets with the free-voice.

Example 8.5. WAS GOTT TUT, Melody in left hand, right hand free with triplets.

➤ STEP 4: Same melody, sixteenth notes in the free voice.

Example 8.6. WAS GOTT TUT, Melody in left hand, right hand free with sixteenth notes.

In this step you will most likely have a lot of runs, arpeggios, patterns and sequences. This is okay, but be sure that sequences and patterns are not eternal, and that you balance the use of runs and arpeggios.

➤ STEP 5: Same melody, combining all the various rhythmic values previously used in the free voice.

Example 8.7. WAS GOTT TUT, Melody in left hand, right hand free combining all the note values so far.

This entire process can be repeated, placing the melody in the right hand and the free voice in the left hand. This too, might seem difficult at first, but it is an excellent skill to develop.

APPLIED HARMONIES

If you have been doing the above steps for some time, you may be looking for a drink with a different flavor: some new and interesting harmonies to represent in your counterpoint.

Consider adding "applied dominants" (see p. 113). This will sound wonderful through the accidentals that applied harmonies produce. Accidentals are amazingly refreshing.

Example 8.8. WAS GOTT TUT, Free voice adding "applied" harmony notes. Refreshing!

You can introduce any of the techniques for discovering new harmonies discussed in the previous chapter to bring interest into the counterpoint. Think a harmony, then flesh it out with the free-voice line.

THREE PARTS—for the brave

If steps one through five are beginning to be too easy, and you have a feel for exploring applied harmonies, you are ready for more of a challenge: working with three voices.

➤ Step 1: Melody in the right hand, a free voice in the left hand, and a free voice in the pedal—one note per melody note.

No, we're not talking about a Bach three-part trio sonata. But the word *trio* does fit.

Example 8.9. Tune: WAS GOTT TUT, attr. Severus Gastorius, c. 1675.
Melody in right hand, left hand and pedal free with quarter notes.

➤ Step 2: Eighth notes in left hand, pedal and melody quarter notes.

Example 8.10. Tune: WAS GOTT TUT, Melody in right hand, left hand free with eighth notes, pedal free with quarter notes.

➤ Step 3: Triplets in left hand; pedal and melody quarter notes.

Example 8.11. Tune: WAS GOTT TUT, Melody in right hand, left hand free with triplets, pedal free with quarter notes.

➤ Step 4: Sixteenth notes in left hand; pedal and melody quarter notes.

Example 8.12. Tune: WAS GOTT TUT, Melody in right hand, left hand free with sixteenth notes, pedal free with quarter notes.

➤ Step 5: Sixteenth notes in left hand; eighth notes in pedal; quarter notes for melody.

Example 8.13. WAS GOTT TUT, Melody in right hand, left hand free with sixteenth notes, pedal free with eighth notes.

➤ Step 6: Mix them all up!

As with two-part counterpoint, you can repeat all the steps and put the melody in the left hand, and the free voices in the right hand and pedal. Then, if you are feeling especially adventurous, repeat them again, putting the melody in the pedal.

FOUR PARTS–for the experienced

Four-part counterpoint is slightly expanded four-part harmonizations, with greater attention given to inner lines. Are the inner lines interesting? It is possible to "set" up the ears to hearing the inner voices by small introductions before the melody begins, bringing in one voice at a time.

Example 8.14. A four-part chorale prelude on "How Dry I Am."

When I was studying counterpoint with Ernst Pepping in Berlin, Germany, he would often get irritated while looking at the assignments and say "Ja, you followed the rules here, but it has to sound ***beautiful!***" Then he would take his red pen and dramatically cross out monotonous sections. When we begin noticing how the inner voices sound as lines themselves, we will be on the way to maturity!

Enough exercises. Let's start putting pieces together: form!

Chapter 9

HARMONY AND COUNTERPOINT TOGETHER:

Creating FORMs

Chapters 7 and 8 of this section dealt with developing abilities: harmonizing tunes and working with tunes in counterpoint.

You've shaved the mud off and have rough jewels. Now let's polish them and give them a setting. Let's put them all together, adding some forms that can be used in our responsibilities as leaders of congregational song.

When the imagination cannot come up with a free-form improvisation, it is extremely helpful to have a skeleton to build on musically. A compositional form provides this. Sometimes working with a form will lead to another musical thought that stretches beyond the form, or that is even completely unrelated. Sometimes the form is exactly right in its pure sense. Musical forms are helpful both as frameworks for musical thought and as catalysts for the imagination.

Preparation for improvising in specific forms needs solid work in harmony and counterpoint. 1) Play and harmonize in several different keys the hymn you intend to use. Not only does this prepare you to do the ever-so-important act of GETTING OUT OF TONIC when you are creating pieces based on these hymns, it ensures that you are very familiar with the hymn. It will be solid in your fingers, with its harmonic progressions and possibilities. Once you are comfortable playing a hymn in several keys, you are clearly ready to open many doors. 2) Go through the two-part counterpoint steps in the previous chapter. Your fingers will discover counterpoint possibilities, and the hymn will sink deeper into your soul.

In this chapter you will find a miscellany of SOME forms to apply to your work in improvisation. The list of forms I have included here is by no means exhaustive. I feel that these tools are good starting points for people developing improvisatory skills. Unlike chapters 7 and 8, the exercises provided here are not necessarily sequential. You can jump around and study them as you need. Like many of the lists in this book, consider this list just the beginning of your own.

TWO-VOICE "RITORNELLO"

In this form a musical idea is developed that is reiterated in one voice between each phrase of a hymn tune in the other voice. Over many years of workshops and private teaching I have arrived at another plan for developing ritornellos.

◆ **Step 1:** Develop a rhythmic counterpoint to the first phrase of a hymn. Do this by tapping the rhythm of the melody with a foot, and clapping an interesting rhythm against it. Syncopation is good. Playing opposites is good. If the melody has long note values, the counterpoint uses short values and vice-versa. Thus:

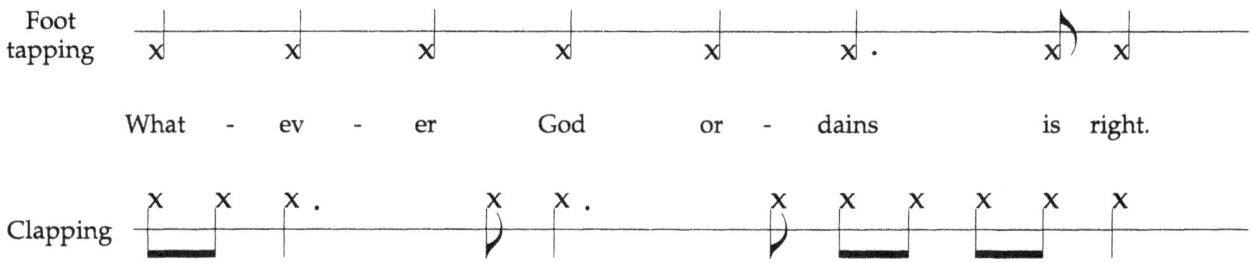

This step usually happens by going over and over and over the phrase while trying out rhythms against the melody's rhythm, each time getting closer to repeating the same rhythm more than once. Eventually you will settle into playing the rhythmic counterpoint the same each time.

◆ **Step 2:** Put notes to this rhythmic counterpoint for the opening phrase—notes that work melodically in counterpoint to the melody. Continue playing opposites: if the melody starts low, start the counterpoint high. If the melody goes up, counterpoint goes down. Then add a two measure answer to your newly devised countermelody.

Example 9.1. Developing a ritornello. Tune: WAS GOTT TUT, Severus Gastorius, c. 1650–c.1693.

◆ **Step 3:** Play the counterpoint you have arrived at in steps 1 and 2 all by itself. Is it interesting? If not, start over. If so, try it in other keys. Try it in minor.

Example 9.2. Ritornello in other keys: sub-dominant (B-flat), dominant (C), and relative minor (D minor).

◆ **Step 4:** Now we are going to insert this ritornello between each phrase of the hymn. It will need to be in a different key each time (even though each phrase of the melody of the hymn will always be played in its key). Only use the key of the hymn for the first statement of the ritornello and after the last phrase. In between, it can be anywhere *but* that key.

To figure out which keys you will use for these ritornello interludes, go back to the entire hymn tune you are working with. What is the ending note of each phrase? What harmony can go with that note other than tonic (the hymn's key itself)? It is good to have one of the statements of the ritornello in the relative key (if a hymn is in a major key, the relative minor, down a third, or if the hymn is in a minor key, the relative major, up a third), and there is almost always a place to state the ritornello in the dominant or sub-dominant. Here's what I mean:

Example 9.3. WAS GOTT TUT, The last note of each phrase suggests new keys.

◆ **Step 5:** Practice the ritornello alone in these keys.

◆ **Step 6:** Put it together! Here's the map:

A. Ritornello (2 measures with a 2 measure "answer")
B. Left hand plays melody, right hand first two measures ritornello, then free material
C. Right hand ritornello in sub-dominant (B-flat major)
D. Left hand plays second phrase of melody, right hand free
E Right hand ritornello in relative minor (d minor)
F. Left hand plays third phrase of melody, right hand free
G. Right hand ritornello, in dominant (C major)
H. Left hand plays last phrase, right hand free
I. Right hand again plays ritornello in tonic (F major), close

Voilà! Instant piece.

Example 9.4. WAS GOTT TUT, with ritornello interludes. Letters indicate components outlined in step 6 above.

This whole piece evolves from devising a short two measure ritornello and drawing from the skills developed in chapter eight.

TRIO

There is a very similar process for improvising trios. Consider Bach's "Jesu, Joy of Man's Desiring." The opening theme is related to the melody itself, but is counterpoint to the melody when it enters later.

Example 9.5. Tune: WERDE MUNTER, MEIN GEMÜTHE, Johann Schop, c. 1595–1667.
Arrangement: from *Jesu, Joy of Man's Desiring,* Cantata 147, *Herz und Mund und Tat und Leben,* J. S. Bach.

As we see in the Bach example, the first step in trio development is devising a theme that is stated immediately, then followed by free material (perhaps sequence material), followed by the entrance of the hymn tune. Most often this theme can be based on the hymn tune by distorting the rhythm, or using a tiny bit of the melody or a rhythmic motive from the melody itself. In the following example I built the theme on the first nine notes of the hymn tune, then used the last three notes of those nine as the basis for a sequence (a) which leads to another sequence (b). The tune then enters in the tenor, and the right hand delays its reiteration of the theme.

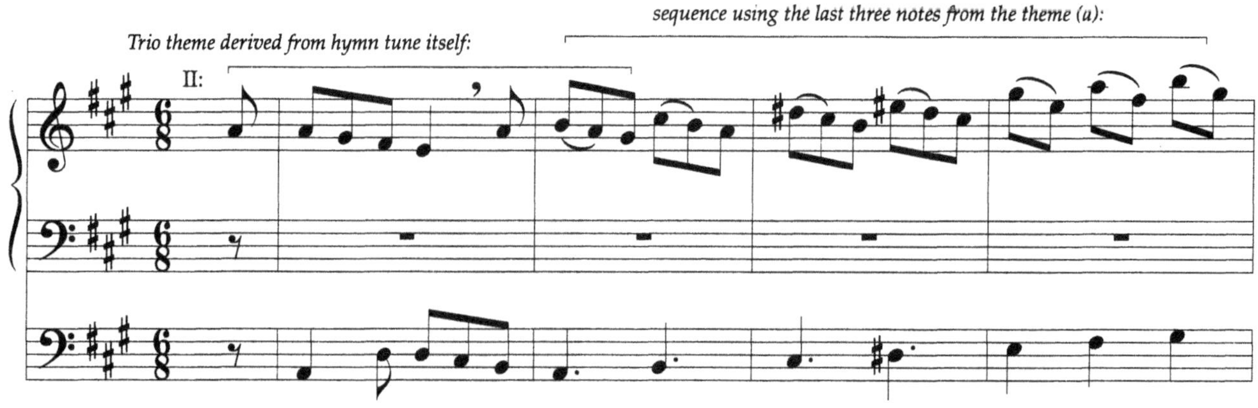

another sequence leading home for tune (b):

Example 9.6. "The Church of Christ in Every Age," Tune: WAREHAM. William Knapp, 1698–1768. Arrangement: David M. Cherwien, *Interpretations Based on Hymntunes, Book VIII.*

It is also possible to build a trio theme that is not at all related to the hymn. It could be a counter melody that you have devised in the ritornello process described above. Your imagination is the only guide you need. Let it roam freely!

COUNTERMELODY

In this particular form, like the ritornello exercises, each phrase of the hymn tune is separated by another accompanied melody. This melody can either be based on the hymn tune, or be completely unrelated. As in the ritornello form, play this countermelody in keys other than the tonic until after the last phrase.

Example 9.7. "From Heaven Above to Earth I Come," Tune: VOM HIMMEL HOCH, V. Schumann, *Geistliche Lieder*, 1539. Arrangement: David M. Cherwien. © 1997. Unpublished.

The following example employs a countermelody that is not based on the tune of the hymn itself:

Example 9.8. "Lord Whose Love in Humble Service," Tune: BEACH SPRING, *The Sacred Harp*, 1884. Arrangement: David M. Cherwien, *Interpretations Based on Hymntunes, Book VII.*

The next example even uses a different hymn tune as the countermelody:

Example 9.9. "Once in Royal David's City," Tune: IRBY, Henry J. Gauntlett, 1805–76.
Arrangement: David M. Cherwien, *Interpretations Based on Hymntunes, Book V.* © 1985. Summa Productions, Minneapolis, MN 55414-1510.

It's a good idea to keep a melody "scrap book." Each time you hum a good two or three measure melody, write it down, put it away for a rainy day. Beethoven kept a notebook in his pocket for this purpose, sketching out little themes that could become an entire symphony. In your case, they can become countermelodies to go with hymns.

ABA FORM

This form is built in three sections, the first and third alike. The progression is simple: a statement (A), branches into different material, perhaps in another key (B), then returns to the familiarity of the opening statement (A) to relieve the stress and tension that venturing into (B) created.

It is a great form for stating the tune of a hymn more than once. It is often the form I will use for the prelude to a service when I wish to have a piece based on a new hymn.

One possible way of working with this form would be to develop a two-part ritornello piece as described above for the (A) section. Then for the (B) section simply play the hymn in its four-part setting (or freely harmonized) in another key—either sub-dominant, dominant, a relative key, or up a major third (my favorite). (If the (A) section is in F major, the (B) section would be in A major. Don't worry much about modulations. In fact I tend to prefer the "lift-drop" method of modulation: lift off the old key, drop onto the new.) After the (B) section, play the entire two-part ritornello again back in the tonic key. Jumping to a new key with a six-four chord (when the fifth is in the bass) seems to emphasize the transition and drives to a new V7-I cadence with what looks like a I six-four-V7-I series of chords. The I six-four chord is actually considered a V chord, and is called a cadential six-four—a kind of V chord with a double suspension.

Example 9.10. An example of a cadential six-four.

However you analyze it, jumping to a new key, or jumping back to the tonic from a distant key with the fifth in the bass is an effective and suspenseful tool.

Another way of creating an A-B-A piece would be to use a melody/countermelody separating phrases as described above, then move to a different key and state the entire hymn without interruption. Then return to the melody/countermelody section. Or, perhaps the B section could be a further development of the countermelody without any mention of the hymn tune.

Countermelody:
I:
mp
3
Melody in left hand:
p
II:
altered for playability
Surprise key!
mf

Example 9.11. "Lord of All Hopefulness," Tune: SLANE, Irish folk tune. Arrangement: David M. Cherwien, *Interpretations Based on Hymntunes, Book VIII.*

FUGAL INTONATION—IMITATION ENTRANCES

This tool uses a portion of the hymn melody—the opening phrase, for example—as a theme or subject for all voices. Fugues begin something like a canon. Each voice enters with the subject in turns. One voice begins by stating the subject, then moves into free material, setting up the next entrance. The next voice usually enters in the dominant key instead of the tonic. The first voice is completely free during the second voice's entrance. A third voice starts back in the tonic as the other two play in counterpoint. It is a wonderful tool, frequently employed by composers.

Example 9.12. "Praise to the Lord, the Almighty," Tune: LOBE DEN HERREN, *Ernewertes Gesangbuch*, Stralsund, 1665. Arrangement: David M. Cherwien, unpublished.

Notice in example 9.12 that when one or two voices move in eighth notes, another voice stops. It is important that each voice gets a turn in moving in eighth notes. It is common to wind up with a static alto line while the soprano and bass take turns moving in eighth notes. Also notice in this example the opposites: contrary motion when possible. Notice how the seventh resolves down and the third up in the final cadence. Notice also how the soprano sets up the dominant C major by creating C major's dominant, G major, signified by the B-natural in measure seven.

This technique can be expanded to four voices.

Example 9.13. "All People That on Earth Do Dwell," Tune: OLD HUNDREDTH, Louis Bourgeois, c. 1510–61.
Arrangement: David M. Cherwien, *Interpretations Based on Hymntunes, Book VIII.*

Imitation can be taken a step further. Each phrase can have a "fugal intonation" as the introduction, basing the themes of these fugal intonations on the notes of the next phrase itself. This is what is done in the next example, with an added twist—the last note of each phrase becomes the new key.

another new key: A major
I:
f
back home to G major!
ff
+Reeds

Example 9.14. "All People That on Earth Do Dwell," Tune: OLD HUNDREDTH, Louis Bourgeois, c. 1510–61.
Arrangement: David M. Cherwien, *Interpretations Based on Hymntunes, Book VIII.*

Another possibility would be to have two voices—one for each hand—that introduce each phrase with imitative entrances. Meanwhile, the melody is played in longer note values by the pedal.

Example 9.15. "At the Name of Jesus," Tune: KING'S WESTON, R. Vaughan Williams, 1872–1958. © Ralph Vaughan Williams, *Enlarged Songs of Praise*, 1931. Reprinted with permission of Oxford University Press. Arrangement: David M. Cherwien, *Interpretations, Based on Hymntunes, Book VI.* © 1987, Summa Productions, Minneapolis, MN 55414-1510.

TOCCATA

In Part One, Chapter 2, I described how to create the toccata. Now if you have spent time with Part Two, Chapter 7, harmonizing with the melody in the pedal, you are one tiny step from an entire piece suitable for a postlude! Instead of playing the four-part harmonization, arpeggiate the same chords with the hands. For variation, continue each phrase in a different key. Just as in earlier harmonization exercises, take the last note of a phrase, imagine what other chord can go with that note and make it a new tonic key for your arpeggios. Then proceed with the melody in the pedal in that key. You may never know where you will end up.

Example 9.16. Toccata on "O Christ Our Light, Our Radiance True," Tune: O JESU CHRISTE, WAHRES LICHT. *Gesang-Buch,* Nürnberg, 1676. Arrangement: David M. Cherwien, unpublished.

Perhaps you could even base the toccata pattern on the hymn tune itself:

Example 9.17. Toccata on "For All the Saints," Tune: SINE NOMINE, Ralph Vaughan Williams, 1872–1958. Taken from *Partita on "For All the Saints,"* by David M. Cherwien. © 1992, Concordia Publishing House, St. Louis, MO.

THERE COULD BE MORE...

I have shared a few of the tricks I keep in my bag. There are many more. Use your own imagination. Build free-form pieces based on motives (little sections of the rhythm or a three-note section of the tune). Expand all of the forms suggested for creating hymn introductions as in Chapter 2.

In Germany students study as far as full thematic trios, fugue (exposition, development, stretto recap, coda), passacaglia and fantasia. The list goes on for quite a while. In that regard, the best teacher for these historic forms would be historic literature.

LEARN FROM LITERATURE

A study of music literature provides an endless flow of ideas for improvisation. How did certain composers work with a particular text and tune? What tricks were in their bag? What key changes did they accomplish, and how? By looking at literature and the techniques of composers past and present, we can open new doors for our own improvisation.

Let's look at a few examples, to give an idea of what kinds of things to look for:

Example 9.18. Chorale prelude: "Ich ruf zu dir," *Orgelbüchlein*. J. S. Bach.

This prelude is one of the most beautiful simple pieces. Notice that if reduced, this piece might just as well have been:

Example 9.19. Reduced, Bach's setting of "Ich ruf zu dir" seems fairly simple.

Bach gently pulses the pedal notes, gently arpeggiates the left hand harmonies, and embellishes the tune slightly. Try this with "Beautiful Savior."

Example 9.20. "Beautiful Savior," using Bach's "Ich ruf zu dir" accompaniment.
Tune: SCHÖNSTER HERR JESU, Silesian folk tune, 1842.

Another Bach *Orgelbüchlein* piece demonstrates an accompaniment motive:

Example 9.21. Chorale prelude: "Herr Christ, der ein'ge Gottes Sohn," *Orgelbüchlein*, J. S. Bach.

In example 9.21, "Herr Christ, der ein'ge Gottes Sohn," Bach makes use of a motive. Notice the pedal line. The alto and tenor set up this motive, and the pedal makes full use of it. Try this technique with "Now Thank We All Our God".

Example 9.22. "Now Thank We All Our God," using the same motive from Bach's "Herr Christ, der ein'ge Gottes Sohn." Arrangement: David M. Cherwien.

Do you see anything "falling" in the next Bach *Orgelbüchlein* piece?

Example 9.23. Chorale prelude, "Durch Adam's Fall ist ganz verderbt," *Orgelbüchlein,* J. S. Bach.

Bach takes the word "fall" and puts it into the music. The alto and tenor seem to fall continuously, as does the motive in the pedal, falling a chromatic seventh interval. (Bach often represented sin with falling chromatics.)

The next two examples show thematic entrances:

Example 9.24. Chorale prelude : "Vom Himmel hoch, da komm ich her," Friedrich Wilhelm Zachau.

Example 9.25. Chorale prelude: "Wie schön leuchtet der Morgenstern," Johann Pachelbel.

Notice in both examples 9.24 and 9.25 how each voice imitates the melody before the tune is stated in half notes.

I dare you to improvise something like this:

Example 9.26. Chorale prelude: "Lobt Gott, ihr Christen alle gleich," Helmut Walcha. © 1963 Henry Litolff's Verlag, C.F. Peters, Frankfurt, London, New York. Taken from *Choralvorspiele für Orgel*, Peters Edition, #4871.

This very complex chorale prelude states the melody-derived theme in each voice of the accompaniment stretto (overlapping) in cascading dominants: first voice in F, then C, then G, then D. The melody of the hymn is played by octaves in the right hand. Unbelievable. I can almost see words blinking across the screen: "Do not try this at home!"

If you feel you are beginning to run out of ideas for your improvisation, it is time to pull out the chorale prelude literature and do some study. Buxtehude, Bach, Pachelbel, Walther, Mendelssohn, Brahms, Karg-Elert, Distler, Pepping, Walcha, Dupré, Manz, to name a few, have all published literature based on the church's songs. Learn from them. Imitate. Through imitation you can take the important next step: moving into your own style.

CODA

In Part Two of this book I have described exercises for developing improvisation skills, along with ideas and forms with which to shape your ideas.

All the while throughout this book, my hope has been that something will be stimulated—either a new thought, or at least a hunger for new abilities. I hope that the processes I have outlined have been or will be sufficient to get you started, at the same time creating a desire for more.

Ideally, we would have balanced training by the time we begin accompanying the Church's song, learning all the creative arts, as well as re-creating music from the printed page. This means learning from the vast literature and at the same time learning how to create music for our specific situations. There are far too few training programs in the U.S. and Canada that do both. For the most part, you will be on your own in exploring creativity.

There are two wonderful published systems for self-taught improvisation skills that I can recommend for you to go further:

- ◆Hancock, Gerre, *Improvising: How to Master the Art,* Oxford University Press, New York, 1994
- ◆Dupré, Marcel, *Complete Course in Organ Improvisation,* Volumes I, II. Leduc, Paris, 1962

My favorite resource is Marcel Dupré's. I can clearly imagine that if people went through this system of learning, they would be capable of improvising anything—impromptu or prepared. If for no other reason, I have appreciated Dupré's two books for the pages and pages of simple melodies with which to work—first in harmonization, then in creating form pieces. The text of Dupré's books (translated into English from French) is terrifically dense and requires many read-throughs to understand, but both books are well worth it.

When all is said and done, the church's song is simply a vital part of the church's life. Song can unite our hearts and souls as a body of Christ. Songs express that which words alone cannot. And songs will continue to nurture our faith and carry us through both tough and triumphant times.

We are stewards of this song, servants of the Creator. We are meant to be creative and bursting with music.

Go to it.

Index of Examples

Tunes—Alphabetical

Titles—Alphabetical

Miscellaneous Examples

Copyright Holders and Administrators

Abingdon Press
201 8th Avenue South
Nashville, TN 37203

Art Masters Studios, Inc. (AMSI)
1599 8th Street SE
Minneapolis, MN 55414-1510

Concordia Publishing House
3558 S. Jefferson Avenue
St. Louis, MO 63118-3968

The Copyright Company
40 Music Square East
Nashville, TN 37203

William Elkin Music Services
Station Road, Industrial Estate
Salhouse, Norwish, Norfolk
NR 13 6N5
United Kingdom

G.I.A. Publications, Inc.
7404 S. Mason Avenue
Chicago, IL 60638

Hope Publishing Company
380 South Main Place
Carol Stream, IL 60188

The Lutheran World Federation
P. O. Box 2100
Route de Ferney 150
CH-1211 Geneva 2
Switzerland

Paul Manz
Institute of Church Music
1500 W. Belmont Avenue
Chicago, IL 60657-3168

Music Sales Corporation/Shawnee Press
257 Park Avenue South
New York, NY 10010

Oregon Catholic Press
5536 Hassalo
Portland, OR 97213-3638

Oxford University Press
70 Baker Street
London W1M 1DJ
United Kingdom

C. F. Peters Corporation
373 Park Avenue South
New York, NY 10016

Walton Music Company
170 NE 33rd Street
Ft. Lauderdale, FL 33334

Paul Westermeyer
Luther Seminary
2481 Como Avenue
St. Paul, MN 55108